Think-Ability

An Operating Manual for Your Mind

Professional Thinking Partners

Overview of Think-Ability

Chapter I:
Personal Thinking Patterns: the History   6

Chapter II:
The Three Different Brain Waves: Beta, Alpha, Theta   8

Chapter III:
Percepetual Triggers: Visual, Auditory, Kinesthetic   16

Chapter IV:
Putting It All Together   34

Chapter V:
Profiles of the Six Thinking Patterns   36

Chapter VI:
Frequently Asked Questions   72

Chapter VII:
About PTP; Our Programs and Products   77

About this Manual

Professional Thinking Partners--a consulting firm based in Park City, Utah--has worked with global and national corporations, non-profits, government organizations, and school systems over the past decade to help maximize the diversity of talent within individuals, teams, and companies. Understanding diversity of thinking enables people to identify their unique strengths and gifts, and see how they can best deliver those gifts. This understanding fosters better communication, enhanced learning and leadership development, and improved team dynamics and organizational effectiveness.

The information in this handbook on Personal Thinking Patterns is the foundation of Professional Thinking Partners' work. It is focused on the "hardware" of your brain--how your brain processes information. A second handbook in diversity of thinking will follow, which explores Thinking Talents--the "software" of your brain. Other guides will build on this content for specific applications, including business and children.

How Think-Ability will help you:

**Understand your own learning process
and that of others.**

**Gain a new perspective on why breakdowns
between people occur, and increase your options
of how to respond.**

**Perform your best by maximizing the
conditions of your own learning and communication.**

**Increase effectiveness in connecting with
a diversity of thinking and working patterns.**

**Learn how to shift from focused to
innovative thinking, and back.**

**Gain awareness and respect for different
modes of thinking.**

Chapter I

Personal Thinking Patterns: the History

Personal Thinking Patterns represents the life work of Dr. Dawna Markova, a noted author and thought leader who has specialized in the fields of learning, perception, and communication for over 40 years. Her model is a distillation of years of research and was influenced by a variety of different fields including psychology, hypnotherapy, anthropology, education, and neuroscience. Her work has been used around the world in schools, businesses, health-care and government agencies.

In her research and discovery of Personal Thinking Patterns, Dr. Markova synthesized the work of 1) E. Roy John, who was revolutionizing brain-wave study at New York University in the 1970's; 2) Edward Hall, an anthropologist who wrote *Beyond Culture*; and 3) Dr. Milton Erickson, an M.D. and hypno-therapist with whom she studied for 23 years. While student teaching in Harlem as a learning specialist, Dr. Markova began to notice how certain children struggling in the school system simultaneously exhibited near-genius levels of competence at other activities outside the classroom. She experimented with multi-modal teaching, transferring students' patterns of success to the domains of learning in which they were having difficulty. For example, one child who had been unable to learn to read (this school taught reading by the phonetic approach) was also the school chess champion. In less than a year, Dr. Markova helped him become an adept reader by following his approach to playing chess. In short, rather than blaming or labeling a child, Dr. Markova achieved success by matching her teaching style to the child's natural pattern of intelligence.

Developing and refining this discovery further over several years in various school systems, universities, and clinical practice, Dr. Markova discovered that six distinct thinking patterns emerge. This book explores those patterns, offers background information, and more importantly, describes what this knowledge can mean for each of us: for parents in helping their children, for the children themselves, as well as for individuals, couples and groups wishing to improve their learning and performance in any domain of human endeavor.

This methodology helps us understand how people think and learn differently. It can enable us to use our own unique thinking pattern and relate more effectively with the people around us. This model does not define personality; it is not meant to label people or "put them in a box." It focuses entirely on the way we perceive information, and how that affects the ways we think, learn, and communicate. Therefore, we hope that this information is used to liberate and expand human capacity.

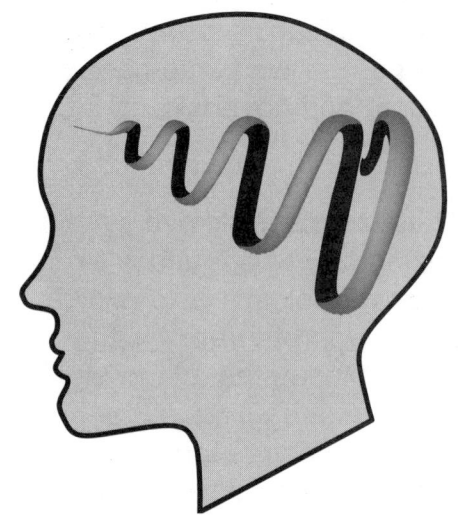

The Thinking Spiral

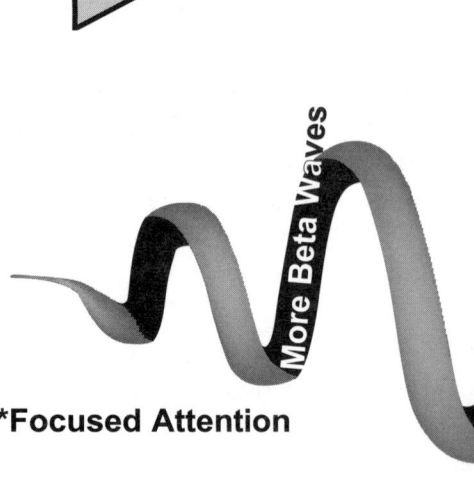

More Beta Waves

More Alpha Waves

More Theta Waves

*Focused Attention

*Detailed Thinking

*Wider Attention

*Exploratory Thinking

*Expanded Attention

*Innovative Thinking

Chapter II

The Three Different Brain Waves

We all assume that people think in the same way. But Dr. Markova's research shows that there are at least six possible ways that people take in information and express themselves. What we will uncover in this chapter--the various states of thinking, the way thought is metabolized in the brain to organize, sort, and generate new ideas from your experience--is the first step to becoming intelligent about your particular thinking patterns.

As far as neuro-science can prove now, the waking mind produces three kinds of brain waves: **beta**, **alpha**, and **theta** waves. (The states of mind that these waves produce have traditionally been called *conscious, subconscious*, and *unconscious*). To make the flow of thought through these states visible, we'll follow the logic of a spiral. Like the beam of a flashlight, your attention covers a wider area of possibilities, becoming more and more divergent as you open your mind to expand your consciousness.

Starting at the center point, you are conscious of a thought: attentive, focused, concentrating, linear and detail-oriented. Here your brain is producing mostly **beta** waves.

As you relax your mind, and the thought begins to digest, your attention becomes more diffuse. This is where you are sifting and sorting; where you might experience yourself as confused or wondering or perplexed or slightly mind-wandering. Here your brain is generating mostly **alpha** waves.

As the thought becomes integrated, stored, and shaped into new patterns, your attention becomes the most diffuse of all. The spiral is now fully open and expanded, and you are "lost in thought." In this cradle of your innermost awareness, your brain is generating mostly ***theta*** waves. You grow more and more receptive in order to access the most innovative and generative aspects of your brain.

As thought moves wider and wider in the spiral, it becomes more symbolic, more receptive, more intuitive, more sensitive, and more private. And you are less aware of it; less able to concentrate on just one thing. If you communicate from the widest place in the spiral, what comes out may be inspired and rich in imagery, but it may also be confusing to others or seem very circular and abstract, lacking the details that make it coherent.

Beta, Alpha, and Theta Waves

*In these graphs, *External attention* refers to everything you perceive in the external world around you. *Internal attention* refers to everything you experience within yourself: feelings, sensations, your inner voices and visions.

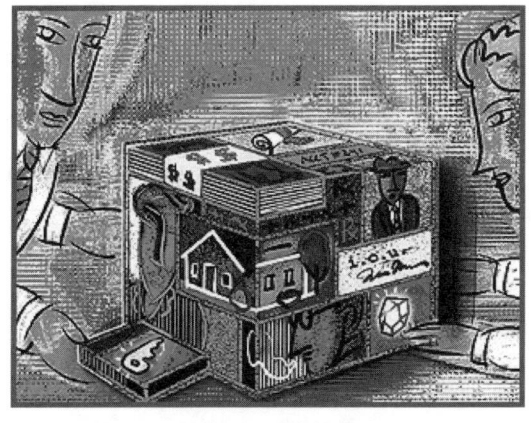

More beta waves
analysis, detail, decision, focus
External attention.

More alpha wave
sorting, confusion, indecisive
External & internal attention.

More theta waves
synthesis, spaced-out, generating,
innovating, creating;
majority of thoughts are symbols
Internal attention.

Characteristics of More Beta Waves

Alert

Organized

Sequential

Decisive

Analytical

Stable

Clear

Linear

Detailed

Active

Focused

Convergent

"Public"

Ordered logic

Externally oriented

Detailed Description of Beta Thinking

When your brain is producing mostly beta waves, it's like the focus of a laser beam. This is a person's most expressive state. Here thoughts can be readily retrieved or recalled. Here, we tend to be more confident, but also more critical. This is the state of mind that most people use to think in a linear, logical, rational, "reasonable" way. This is commonly referred to as left-brained thinking. This is where we are most comfortable and competent receiving information and expressing ourselves in public, and where we are the least distractable.

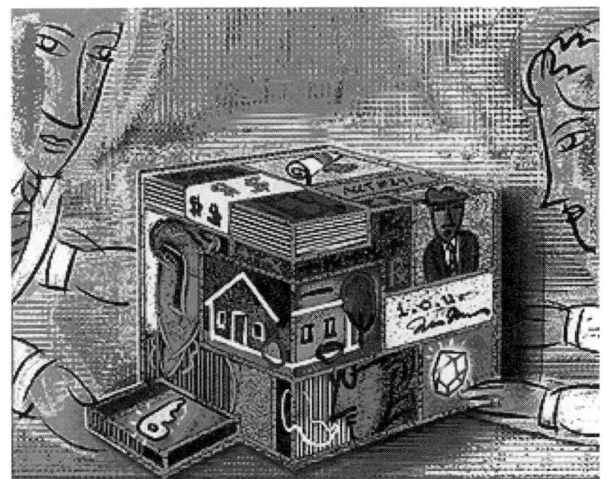

When the brain produces mostly beta waves, we are the most alert and the least receptive. This state of mind is the home of the tried and true, because it loves routines, rules, details, and orderly things that behave as expected. Its purpose is separation and discrimination. Thus everything becomes partitioned into objectified units.

This is where patterns are memorized; once familiar, these are used to make decisions in unfamiliar situations. If you come upon an unknown object in the road, hear a strange sound in the night, or smell something unrecognizable, your mind will use the beta mode to identify what it is and why it is there. This is what prevents you from sticking your hand in the fire over and over, and makes it possible not to need to experiment with each new danger before avoiding it.

Linear
Sequential
Most alert
Easy to express
Least distractable

Beta

© PTP, INC.

11

Characteristics of More Alpha Waves

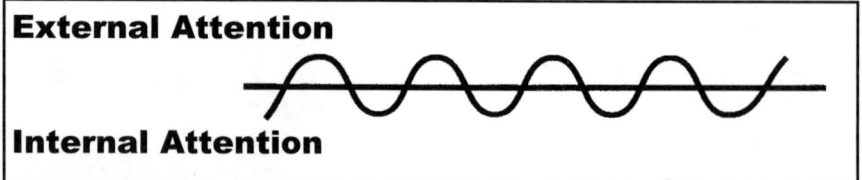

Confused

Considering

Sorting

Comparing

Exploring

Separating and bridging

Some symbolic thinking

Detailed Description of Alpha Thinking

When the brain is producing mostly alpha waves, it is in an in-between state: the revolving door of our minds where the vast array of input we receive from the outer world is sorted. It is a transitional way of thinking, for here the brain is metabolizing information and exploring options. It is a state of mind that is engaged by experimentation and resists too much external structure. It is thinking in dualities, a two-way mode: "Either I do this or that; either his side of the story is right or hers is right; either I see it this way or that way."

This type of thinking is vital for decision-making and image-making, for it is the bridge between our inner and outer worlds. Recognizing and acknowledging this makes it easier to expand when we're "confused," giving our brains the time they need to cross that bridge comfortably. Alpha thinking functions as a threshold where our inspiration and wisdom are distilled before being expressed. It is a domain that is both public and private, receptive and active; between our interior and exterior minds, where we are motivated into action and soothed into relaxation.

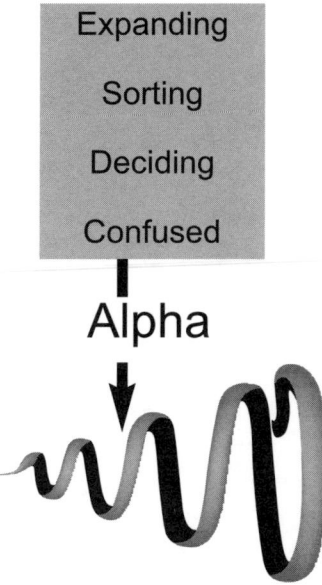

Characteristics of More Theta Waves

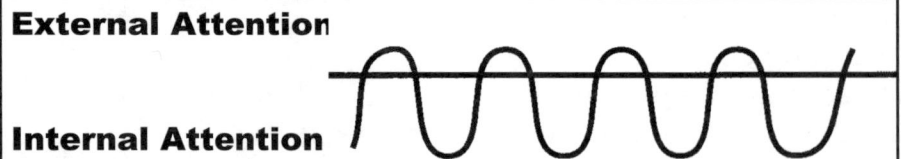

Imaginative

Generative

Creating new patterns

Synthesizing

Connective

Brainstorming

Receptive

Divergent

Blue-Skying

Mostly symbolic thinking

Finding meaning

Web thinking

"Private"

Relational logic

Intuition

Detailed Description of Theta Thinking

To explore theta thinking, allow yourself to remember a time you really spaced out and were lost in your thoughts. Perhaps driving on a highway at night when you were at exit 15, then suddenly you noticed you were at exit 19? What happened to exits 16, 17 and 18? Who was that masked person driving your car?

This is a time of taking a brief mental vacation. Your thoughts go wide and receptive, and often very deep. You probably learned to apologize for thinking this way in school, for "daydreaming," and not paying attention to the teacher. In fact, in this state, your brain was processing what you were learning, searching internally for how the new information fit with what you already had experienced, making new patterns from it, storing information for the long term, and dreaming new possibilities for the future. Here you think about the way things *could be*.

In theta, the brain thinks in many ways at once, as if in a web, creating and carrying messages indirectly through dreams, symbols, and imagery. Because it can think in so many directions simultaneously, this mode enables us to be alive in the contradictions that challenges offer. It searches for the pattern that will reveal the whole of something, the forest rather than the trees. Theta is the mode of thought most capable of understanding the whole of something, the big picture. This is the place of deepest spiritual connection and healing, of that elusive inner voice or insight, gut feeling and intuition.

Synthesizing
Generating
Pattern seeking
Innovative
Most distractable

Theta

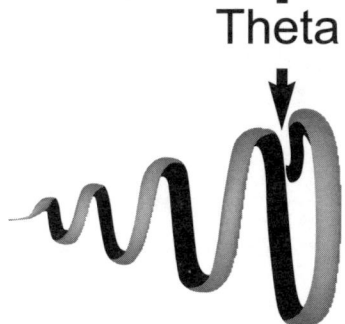

© PTP, INC.

Chapter III

Perceptual Triggers

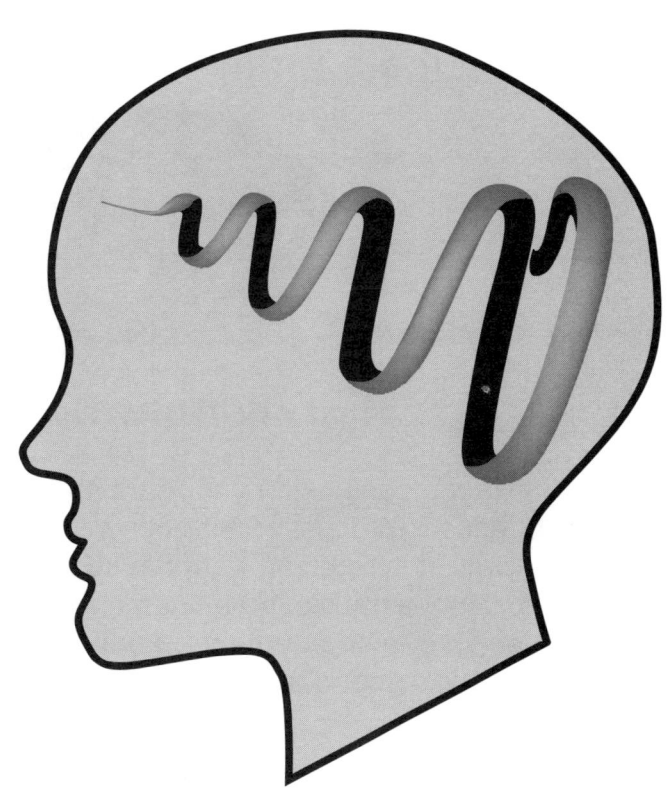

Each of us takes in the world through three perceptual channels: auditory, visual, and kinesthetic. In this chapter you will discover which of these stimuli triggers your mind to produce more beta, alpha, and theta waves.

Auditory

Listening • Telling
Discussing • Singing • Talking

What AUDITORY Thinking Means:

Auditory thinking means using your ears and mouth as the telephone of your mind. Experience is processed through words and sounds. When your mind is thinking this way, it is listening to and participating in conversations, tones of voice, jokes, sounds, music, meanings and messages, poems, stories, debates, speeches, lectures, and arguments. Auditory creativity involves expressing consciousness with sound and/or words.

The active and receptive modes of auditory

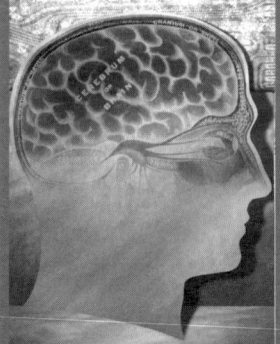

Receptive:

Listening
Being told
Radio
Music

Active:

Storytelling
Lecturing
Singing
Telling jokes
Selling
Discussing
Speaking

Visual

Looking • Watching • Reading
Showing • Observing
Writing • Drawing

What Visual Thinking Means:

Visual thinking means using your eyes and "insight" as the windows of your mind. Experience is processed through sight and visual images. When your mind is thinking this way, it is observing visual details, colors, visions, lines, maps, lists, views, perspectives, visualizations, drawings, the written word, diagrams, movies, charts, television, and photographs. Visual creativity involves setting ideas to paper, canvas, computer, or film.

The active and receptive modes of visual

Receptive:

Watching
Reading
Illustration
Being shown

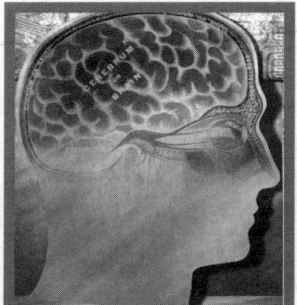

Active:

Writing
Editing
Drawing
Films/video

© PTP, INC.

Kinesthetic

Doing • Moving • Feeling
Hands-On • Sports • Making

What Kinesthetic Thinking Means

Kinesthetic thinking means functioning through hands, skin, and muscles. Experiences are collected in feelings, movements, actions, touch, texture, temperature, pressure, spatial awareness, sensitivity to energy, and smell. Kinesthetic creativity involves using hands and bodies to sculpt, garden, dance, carve, cook, build, etc.

The active and receptive modes of kinesthetic

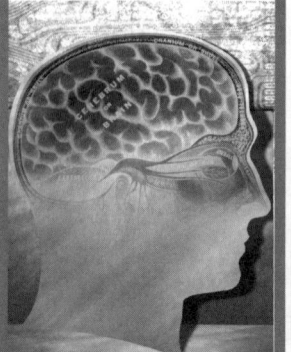

Receptive:

Smelling
Tasting
Feeling
Sensing
Physical environment

Active:

Sports
Hands-on
Building
Doing
Moving
Demonstrating

Everyone uses and experiences all three modes. What distinguishes the patterns is the order in which they trigger the different brain wave states.

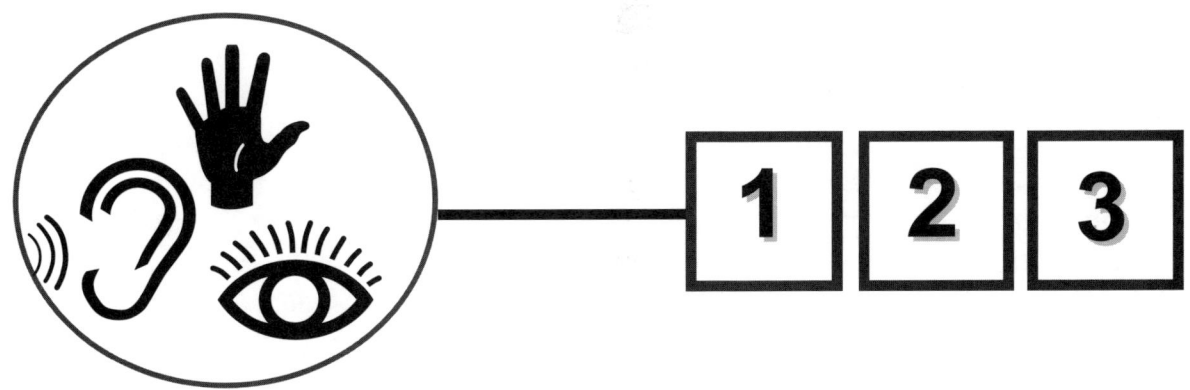

What Do You Know About Your Thinking?

In which mode is it easy for you to be active or receptive (visual, auditory, or kinesthetic)?

In which mode is it difficult to be active publically?

In which mode can you express for long periods and not get tired?

In which mode are you most shy and sensitive?

The next nine pages present a detailed look at what it means to have visual, auditory, and kinesthetic trigger someone into the three different states of mind.

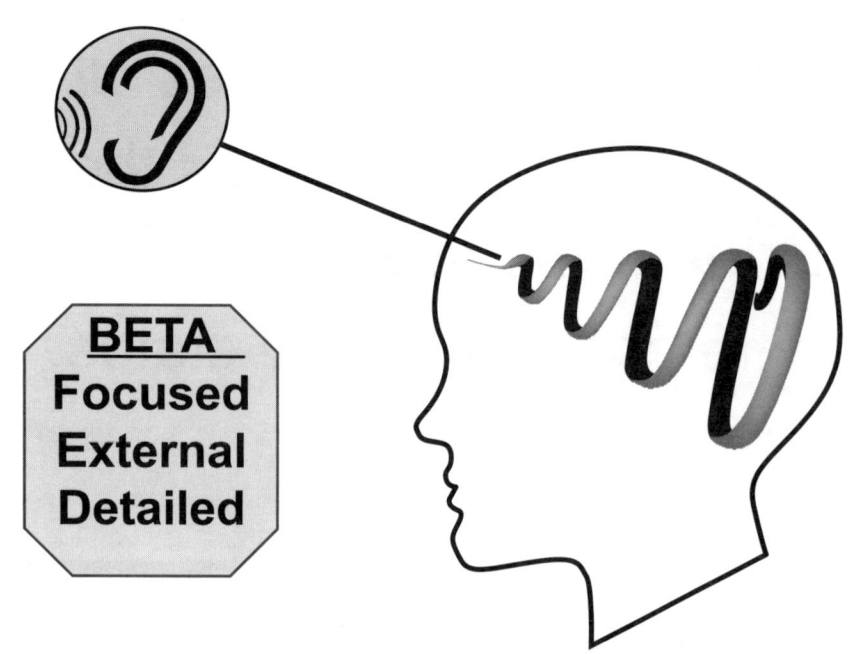

BETA
Focused
External
Detailed

Auditory in Beta: the Detailed Mind

Learns most easily by discussing

Immediate access of names, what was said

Says things logically, with no hesitation

Describes abstract ideas with complex language

Constant and intense talking

Speaking energizes, brings alert

Verbal contact is casual, natural

Organizes by talking about what needs to be done

Does This Sound Like You?

If auditory triggers you into beta, you might relate to these:

Have you ever known anyone who could talk and talk and talk as if they could go on forever? They use language in very detailed ways. They may speak very quickly. Their vocabulary is often extremely precise. Discussing something seems very customary to them. The first thing they are attracted to when walking into a room is the conversations that are going on. They know you care about them if you discuss things with them, particularly things that matter.

"I can talk to anybody about anything. I talk to people in elevators, on street corners, wherever."

"Do you like to argue? I like to debate, not fight exactly, but philosophically discuss things. I can talk for days about what something means. That's the only way to resolve differences . . . communication is everything. I hate it when someone gives me the silent treatment--it drives me up the wall. I like to process things. As soon as I walk out of a movie, I need to talk about it."

Typical phrases:
"Let me tell you…"
"The verbal headline is…"
"Talk to you later."

Alpha
Sorting
Confusion
Deciding

Auditory in Alpha: the Exploring Mind

Talking helps sort through thoughts

Hears both sides of a story

Metaphors are right beneath the surface

Can hear own inner voice while listening to words on the outside

May hesitate slightly to find words

Can hear the whole as well as details in a conversation

Words are bridges between inner and outer worlds

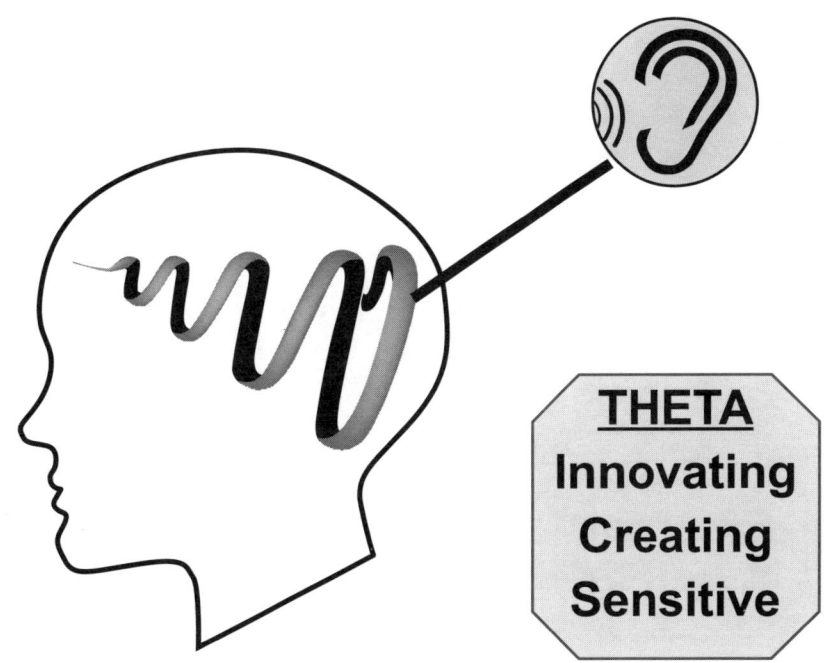

Auditory in Theta: the Innovative Mind

Hears the whole of something

Doesn't like to speak in a detailed way to groups of people

May forget names and initials; words may take a long time to access

Hates to have words filled in by others

Words may be overwhelming

Can hear harmonies internally

Sensitive to tones of voice

Sounds generate ideas; hears things creatively

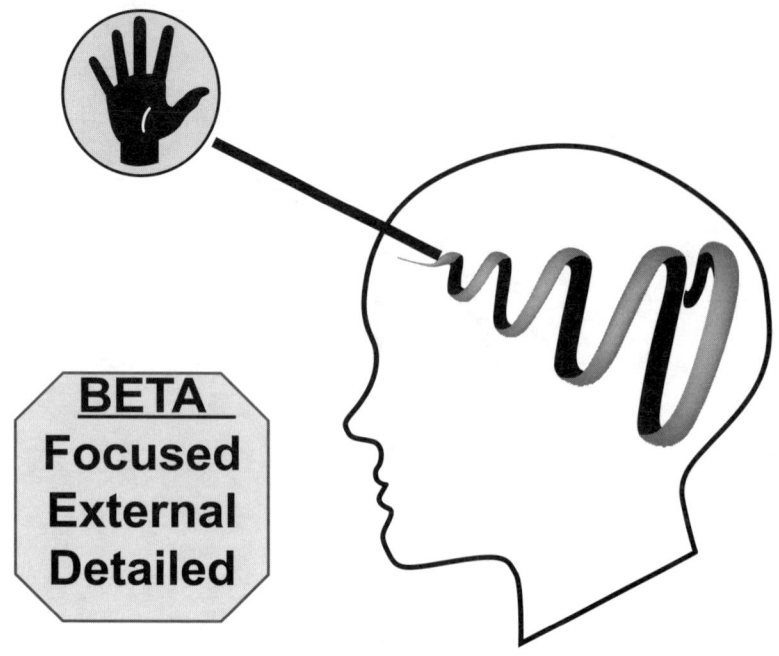

Kinesthetic in Beta: the Detailed Mind

Touch and doing things energizes, makes alert

Organizes in piles and in the systematic way things are done

Learns most easily by doing

Does things logically; likes things concrete

Can spend long periods doing, feeling, touching

Constantly needs to move, jiggle

"*Doing*" is customary

Does This Feel Like You?

If kinesthetic triggers you into beta, you might relate to these:

If this is true for you, you are always game for action. Long meetings where you can't get up and walk around are hard. It's natural for you to just pick up something and start fiddling with it. To make things and put things together is natural. Sports and physical activity are part of your everyday life. If you are going to learn something new you want to try it right away. To read how to do it or listen to instructions can be frustrating unless you can immediately try it. When clothes shopping you tend to have to touch all the materials; you want to be comfortable in what you wear.

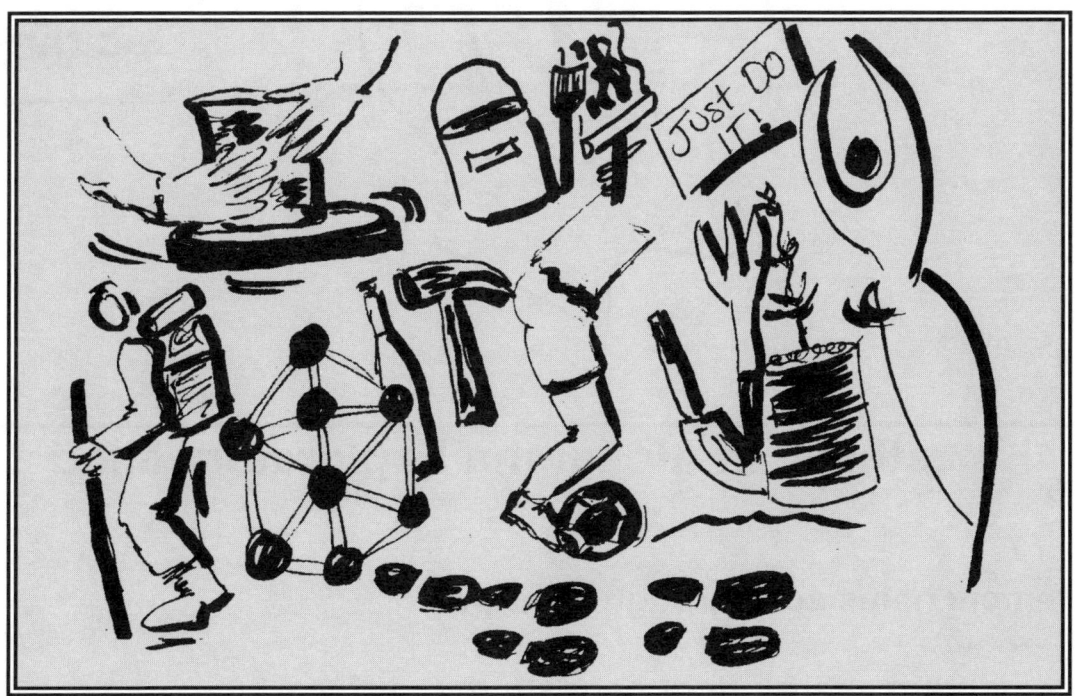

"I love being able to move around my office easily, walking or running helps me center myself."

"People say they have a hard time reading my expression."

"I love organizing my stuff in piles; I can easily sort things or information if I can physically separate it."

Typical phrases:
"Let's cut to the chase."
"I feel like..."
"Catch you later!"

Kinesthetic in Alpha: the Exploratory Mind

Movement helps sort through thoughts

Feels pent-up energy right beneath the surface

Touch and movement are bridges between inner and outer worlds

Feels what they see or hear

Often pulled in two directions

Hand gestures accompany words

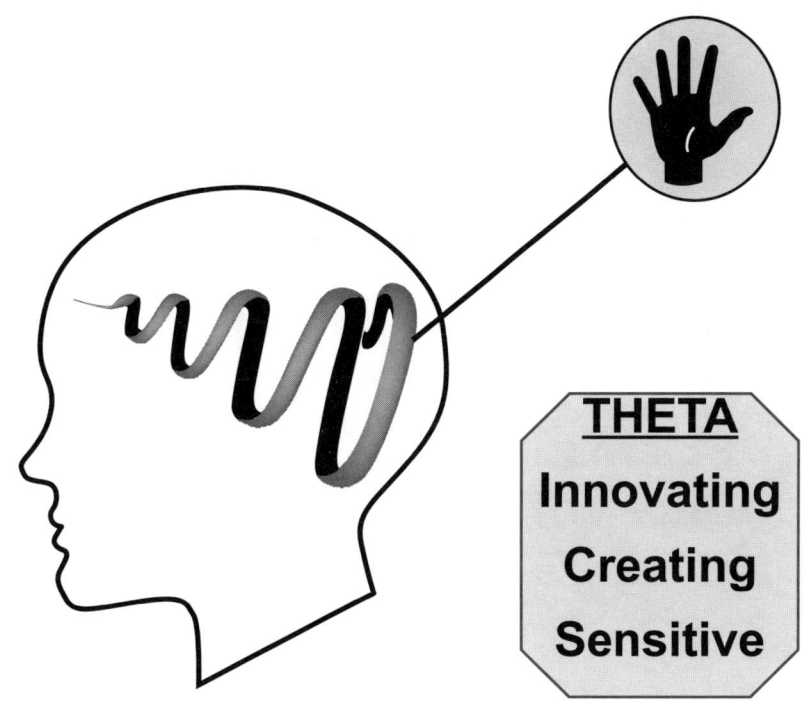

Kinesthetic in Theta: the Innovative Mind

Sensitive, shy to touch

Can sit still and inactive for long periods of time

Does things non-linearly, creatively

Movement generates ideas

Feelings and touch can be overwhelming

Kinesthetic movement entrances

Feels the whole of something

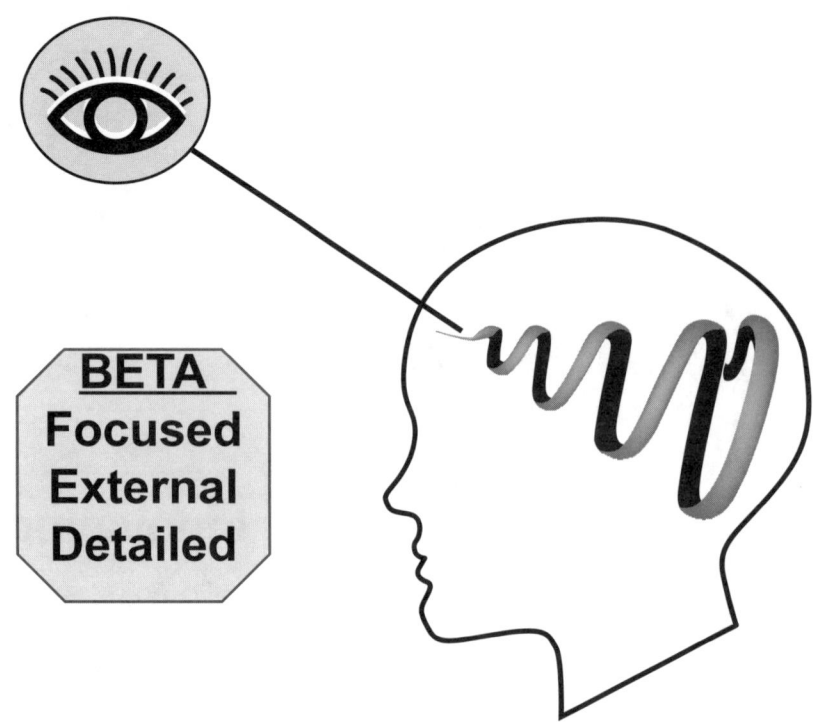

Visual in Beta: the Detailed Mind

Writing, drawing, and looking energizes, makes alert

Organizes by making lists

Learns most easily by reading and watching

Can hold direct and persistent eye contact

Shows and illustrates ideas

Writes things logically

Can work at visual tasks for long periods of time

Showing is customary

Does This Look Like You?

If visual triggers you into beta, you might relate to these:

Those whose beta consciousness is triggered by visual input will constantly look at a person when talking to them. There is persistent eye contact, and facial expressions are very explicit. These people often are very carefully dressed and color co-ordinated. How they look is very important; often they will dress for looks above comfort. Taking notes, doodling, or having accompanying visuals helps them listen. They can read, or watch movies or T.V., exhaustively.

"One of the things that's always been important to me is eye contact. If people don't look at me when I'm talking to them, I feel like they're bored or not listening."

"Color and how things look is everything to me. And I read anything available! Cereal boxes, chewing gum wrappers, faces, graffiti; my eyes never seem to rest."

Typical phrases:
"What does this look like to you...?"
"Picture this:"
"See you later!"

Visual in Alpha: the Exploratory Mind

Writing or drawing helps sort thoughts

Often sees things from two different perspectives

Visions right beneath the surface

Can see visions with eyes open or closed

Has to look to the side to find words

Can see the whole and details

Visions are the bridge between inner and outer world

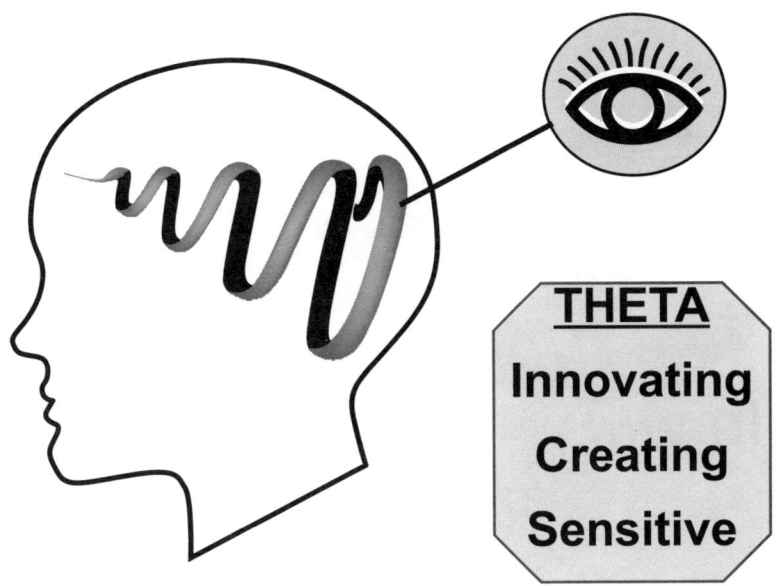

Visual in Theta: the Innovative Mind

Prefers low amount of visual input; too much can overwhelm

Sees the whole of something

Visual input entrances

Dislikes detailed writing, visual diagrams, or instructions

Needs auditory or kinesthetic, not visual, instructions

Shy, sensitive to prolonged eye contact

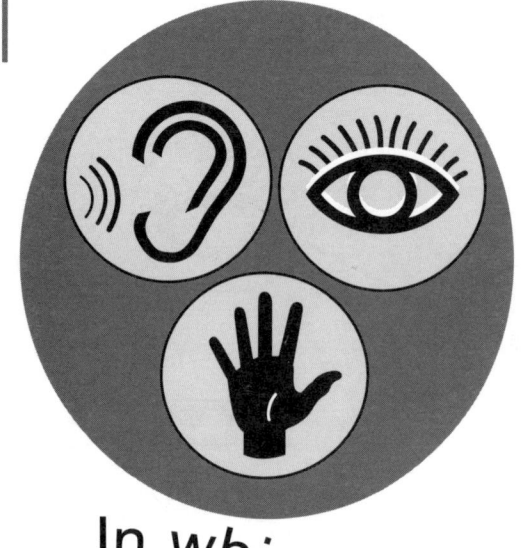

Which of these three triggers:
**auditory,
visual,
kinesthetic**

Produce which brain wave state:
**beta,
alpha,
theta**

in you?

In which order do you use these?

Chapter IV

Putting it All Together

The Thinking Pattern model consists of six different patterns. Some are very different from each other, while others can seem quite similar. What seems easiest for most people is to identify what triggers them into beta first.
As we discovered in the last chapter, each of the three consciousness levels is most sensitive to just one symbolic language. Consequently, there are six possible sequences your brain can use to process information: three possibilities for your conscious mind (Beta), or three different high thresholds as we just experienced. That leaves two for your subconscious mind (Alpha). And that leaves one for your unconscious mind (Theta). Hence, there are six different possibilities:

* Remember that this is the hardware of your brain; it is only about how you process information. It is not about personality!

Exercise to help determine your thinking pattern

Go back through the previous nine pages and mark in this chart which seem most like you. Remember that visual (or auditory, or kinesthetic) cannot trigger you into two states; you should find one page that matches you in visual, one in auditory, and one in kinesthetic page.

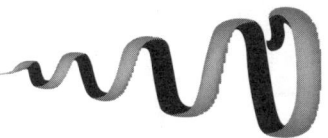

	Beta	Alpha	Theta
Auditory	Auditory Triggers Beta Pg. 21	Auditory Triggers Alpha Pg. 23	Auditory TriggersTheta Pg. 24
Kinesthetic	Kinesthetic Triggers Beta Pg. 25	Kinesthetic Triggers Alpha Pg. 27	Kinesthetic Triggers Theta Pg. 28
 **V**isual	Visual Triggers Beta Pg. 29	Visual Triggers Alpha Pg. 31	Visual TriggersTheta Pg. 32

The Six Thinking Patterns

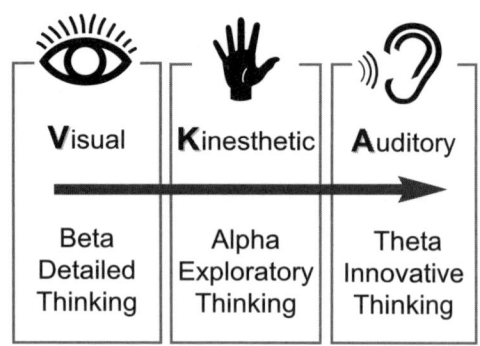

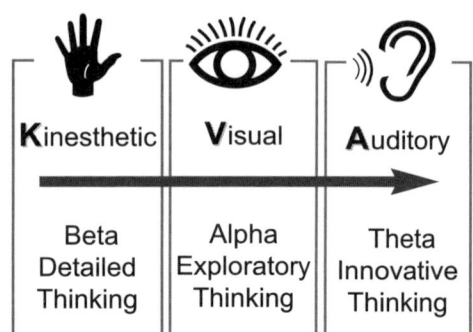

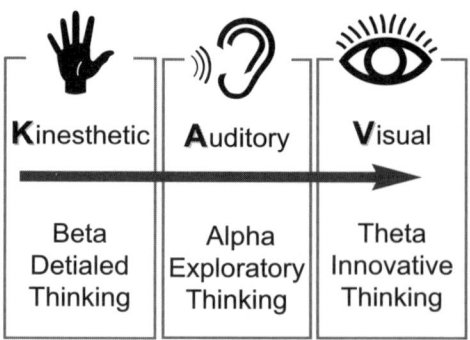

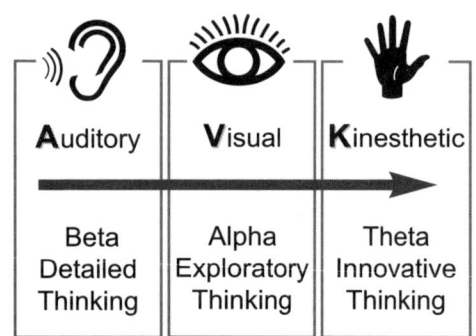

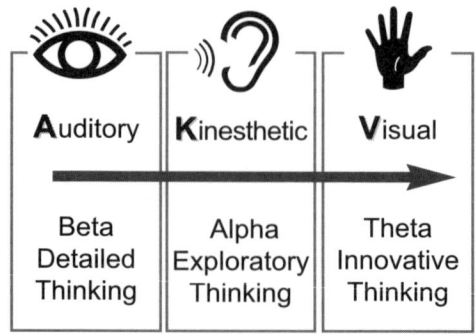

CHAPTER V

Profiles of the Six Patterns

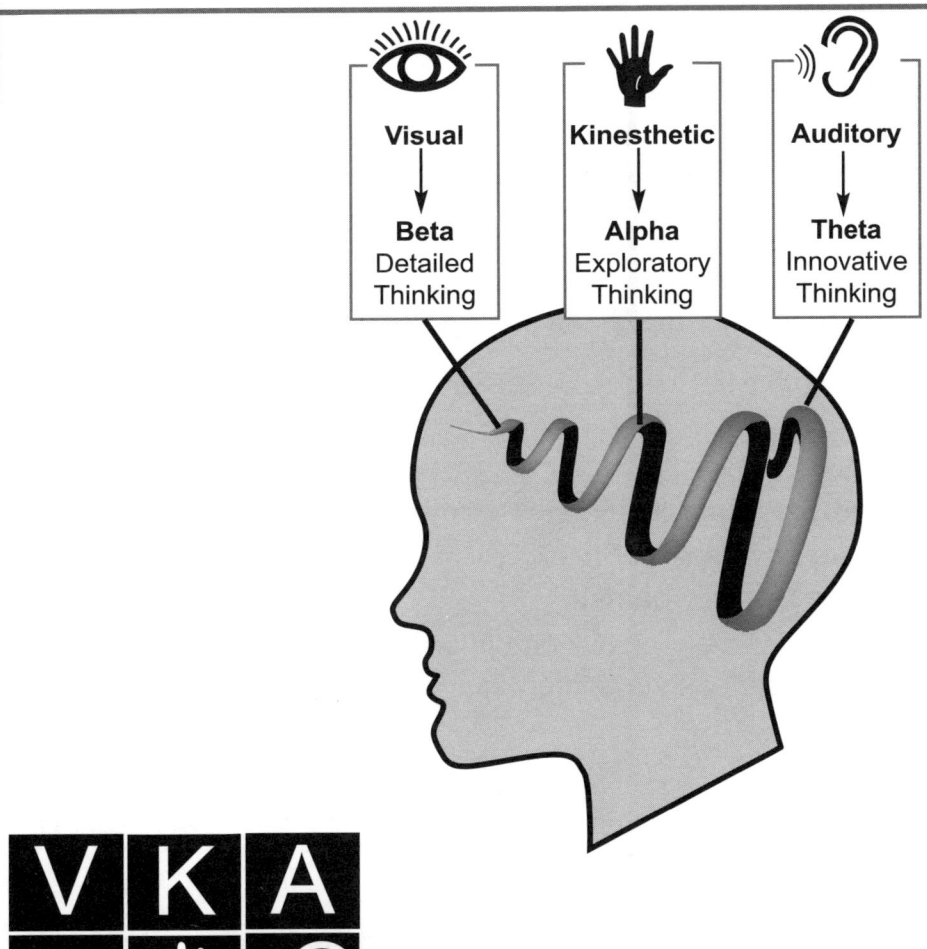

 Characteristics of Your Pattern

People are often struck right away by your visual meticulousness. You are the one that can immediately spot the typo in the 100-page report. How you look is also important to you; you want your clothes, possessions, body, and surroundings to fit an inner image you are trying to create.

You connect with others most easily by making eye contact. You can maintain it steadily, but may have to close your eyes or move to listen in depth. Your eyes are your windows into the world and you have a tendency to feel what you see. You may have pent-up energy right beneath the surface, so physical activity tends to be an important emotional and energetic outlet for you.

You probably enjoy reading, and may like to take extensive notes in meetings and lectures to help remember what you hear.

In large groups, you can be rather quiet. With one or two peers or in small groups, however, you can be very talkative. You may jump from topic to topic, and may not seem to "get to the point," making connections in your speaking that may not be understandable to the listener. Gesturing, moving, or touching helps you find your words.

You may use lots of visual vocabulary--words that paint images and phrases that include "look," "see," "show," "imagine," "I can picture that," or "See you soon." You tend to ask a lot of questions.

Your Natural Gifts and Strengths
- Steady eye-hand and eye-body coordination.
- Remember easily what you have seen or read.
- Can recall faces, but not necessarily names.
- Easily aware of your feelings and the sensations in your body.
- Can pick up the feelings and sensations being experienced by others you see around you.
- May be very physically active.
- Have legible handwriting, good spelling, and proofreading ability.
- May like to draw and design things in detail.
- Easy to write almost word for word what you hear.
- Often prefer to work in groups or on teams rather than independently.
- Hear the whole of something.

Your Challenges
- May be offended by lack of eye contact of others.
- Don't like to speak spontaneously to groups of people.
- May forget names and initials.
- May take a long time to access words.
- Dislike having words filled in by others.
- Sensitive to words and tones of voice.
- Can be difficult to concentrate when required to listen for long periods, or when asked questions about the details of what you've heard.
- May feel pulled in two directions and vacillate a lot before making up your mind.

Best Way to Express Yourself in a Detailed Manner
·You tend to depend on written reminders, lists, instructions, and directions to keep yourself well organized, and it is through writing that you express yourself in the most detailed, organized manner as well.

Best Way to Explore Your Options and Sort Information
·Experience is your best teacher in sorting things out. If you can actually try out the various options, you can then see what is best for you.

Best Way for You to Innovate
·You can get in touch with your innovative capacity through speaking, allowing yourself the freedom to loop and swirl as much as you need while a good listener takes notes and then reads them back to you out loud.

·If you don't have someone to talk to in this way, try getting alone in a room, walking around and talking into a tape recorder and then transcribing your ideas.

Your Most Effective Decision-making Strategies
·The best process to make a decision for you is to write down all the options, then try them out one at a time, then talk about what you discovered to someone who will take down what you say and read it back to you. It may be difficult to make a decision and so it may help if you allow yourself to make a temporary choice, with the freedom to change your mind when it seems right.

·Another option is to try talking with yourself in the mirror to discover what you really want. When you are looking only at yourself, you can know what you want better than when you are around other people.

Your Best Working Environment
·Most likely, you are very particular about the way your physical environment looks; you can't think well with visual clutter and may have trouble in an open office or one with glass doors if you feel you are being looked at all the time.

·You also tend to be very sensitive to auditory distractions and need quiet in order to do your work. You may want to touch base frequently with your team and feel the energy of all the people you are working with around you.

·A lack of visual precision on the part of those you work with can be extremely frustrating. It helps to remember that while this is a strength of yours, others have different abilities.

Your Best Learning Process
·You tend to learn best by watching a demonstration or reading the directions for a task and then experimenting, without being told first how to do it.

·If you get stuck, you might ask questions and want some explanation from others. You do not do well in general, however, with lectures or long, verbal directions, or in discussion groups.

Communicating with Others
·Most likely you are a good communicator one-on-one and in small groups. Try to get very clear about what you think by taking notes before you talk with others; you may find yourself being swayed by others' opinions and agreeing to something you really don't believe in.

·If you must speak in front of a large group, prepare visually in advance, <u>move around to find your words</u>, and draw a chart to keep you on track.

·Suggest to others that they communicate as much as possible with you <u>in writing</u>.

·In meetings, take notes for yourself or volunteer to be the official note-taker standing at a flip chart in order to best remember what was said.

Receiving Feedback
·Since you are auditorily sensitive, it is best to receive negative feedback <u>in writing</u>. Positive feedback can be delivered in writing or verbally along with good eye contact.

·You may want to tell people of other patterns who use sarcasm that you will take in the biting tone of voice and may misunderstand the other person's intention.

Dealing with Conflict
·It is best for you to deal with any conflict <u>in writing or while walking</u>. Otherwise it is easy for you to get swayed by what the other person is saying and go away conceding or agreeing when that is not really true for you.

Receiving Support or Guidance
·Those who wish to give you help or guidance should encourage you to write, to allow your thoughts to come into focus and help you communicate more succinctly.

- Writing is also an effective way for you to express the your feelings.
- Remind others to allow you time to speak and not to finish your sentences, interrupt you, or put words in your mouth.
- Ask others to mirror back to you in words or in writing what you have said.
- You may need to ask a lot of questions. Take notes during phone conversations or in any other important verbal communication, and write down the questions you are currently wondering about. This will help you think for yourself.

The Best Way for You to Relax
- You may need to be encouraged to relax by doing some strenuous physical exercise every day.
- In addition, you may relax most naturally by reading, journaling, and listening to music.

To Enhance Your Physical Well-being
- You really need a physical outlet or you may become very keyed up and tense. Generally you do best doing something with a great deal of intensity--running, skiing, tennis, volleyball--and need to be encouraged to also do some receptive physical practices such as yoga.

Working and Communicating with Other Patterns

 **KVAs**
- KVAs are good work partners for you since you both are auditorily sensitive; you communicate naturally with one another via e-mail and memo, and move smoothly together into action.
- Sometimes, KVAs can be a bit frustrating for you because they work so independently. Be aware that they may not want to interact as much as you do or come to as many meetings as you think are appropriate.

 **KAVs**
- You can also partner well with KAVs, particularly when creating something concrete.
- Be careful not to overwhelm them with visual information--communicate as much as possible verbally, although if you want to praise them, a short e-mail will have a huge impact.
- As much as possible, don't force eye contact--sit next to, not across from, them so their eyes can move where they want to.
- If you find yourself in conflict with a KAV, suggest that you go for a walk to talk it out, and allow them to speak without looking at you.

© PTP, INC.

40

· If you supervise KAV's, allow them to move around in meetings; they will be able to pay attention better and contribute more.

 AKVs

· AKVs may wound you with their verbal sarcasm; try not to take it personally.
· AKVs are visually sensitive, so avoid too much visual information--e-mails, faxes, written memos, visual directions--or a great deal of metaphors.
· Don't draw diagrams when speaking to them, unless you want them to be very innovative in their thinking.
· Allow them not to make eye contact with you.
· If you supervise an AKV, suggest that they get up and move around as they feel inclined, even in meetings; it will enable them to know what really matters to them and have patience with those who speak more slowly.

 AVKs

· AVKs can be challenging to you, because they may overwhelm you with their verbal stamina.
· Remind them, perhaps by a prearranged hand gesture, to leave space so that you can speak; it will not hurt their feelings.
· Encourage them to communicate as much as possible with you via e-mail, or e-mail them and allow them to answer via voice mail.
· Be aware of how difficult it is for them to do any physical task; it is as hard as you getting up in front of 500 people and speaking spontaneously.

VAKs

· People of this pattern meet you naturally in the visual world--sharing images, conversations about movies and books, brainstorming any visual product.
· You naturally communicate best via the written word and through pictures.
· Be aware that VAKs cannot usually do work that is as visually detailed as you do and have trouble estimating well how long a task will take. If you take on those aspects of a project, you both will be happier.

> **Famous people who use the VKA pattern:**
>
> **Princess Diana**
> used this pattern. She always seemed to take in the world through her eyes. Her appearance, rather than her words, seemed of utmost importance. She took action based on what she saw and experienced. She was generally quiet, but what she said seemed to have deep meaning to her.
>
> **Dustin Hoffman**
> uses this pattern. He makes very direct eye contact both in roles and in interviews. When he speaks, the emphasis is more on his tone than what he's saying. He often speaks in questions rather than statements. He seems to have pent-up energy always bursting to get out; he seems most comfortable speaking when he is moving.

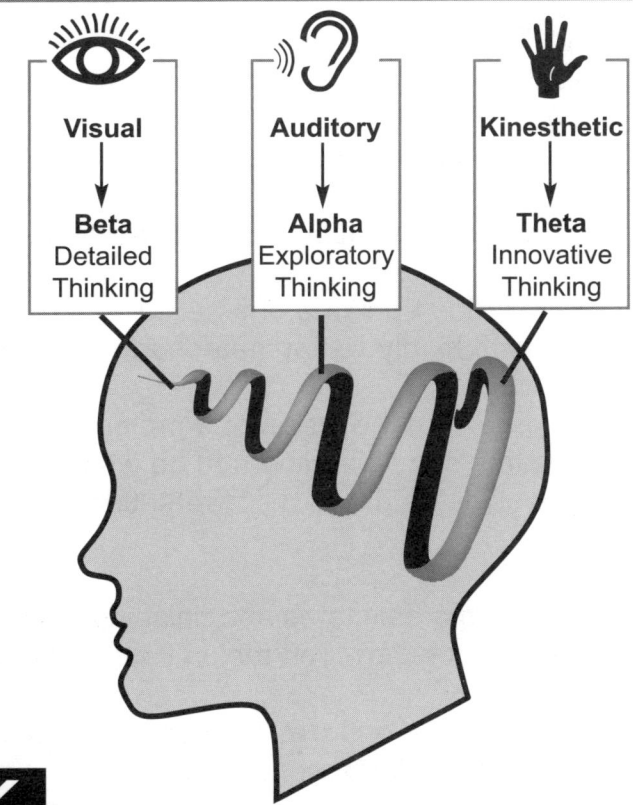

Characteristics of Your Pattern

You are the person who could have invented "Show and tell." You make steady eye contact and like to make a visual impression with the clothes you wear, which are usually colorful, well-coordinated outfits. You love visual details and looking at possibilities: flipping through catalogs, going window shopping, or people-watching. You have the habit of devouring as much as possible of anything in print-cereal boxes, billboards, and books. You can keep a lot of details stored visually, sometimes to the point of having a photographic memory.

Your feelings are written all over your face. In fact, by looking at your face, others may know how you feel before you are even aware of it. You have a lot of feeling behind your words and are often very persuasive in your speaking. You like to teach and explain things, and love to tell stories in great detail, using lots of visual metaphors to paint pictures for your listeners. When you speak, you tend to use visual vocabulary--words like "see," "look," "colorful," "show," and "bright," and phrases like "I can see your point," and "See you later." You often use fillers, such as "um," "like," or "you know," between thoughts.

Your Natural Gifts and Strengths
- Effective teacher and salesperson.
- Love to show and tell.
- Storyteller--love to illustrate ideas with stories.
- Write things logically.
- Excellent visual recall--for faces, what somewhat was wearing, what something looked like.
- Can work at visual tasks for long periods of time.
- Wonderful at coming up with highly visual metaphors to describe situations, people, concepts.
- Can easily hold the big picture or the vision of a project, company, etc.
- Good at weaving stories that convince others to do what they want.
- Can hear the whole as well as details in a conversation.

Your Challenges
- May have difficulty making time estimates and finishing tasks.
- Have to close your eyes to know how you feel in your body, what you want to do, or to move easily.
- Have to do a physical action over and over in order to learn it, and consequently often shy away from hands-on tasks or competitive sports.
- Private about your feelings; touch is not casual for you, so you may be hesitant to make physical contact.
- May be frustrated when others do not make eye contact.
- Can get impatient doing a repetitive activity and may have trouble staying with the same task for a long period of time. To offset boredom, you may go from one activity to another and then back to the first.
- Get confused when given too many choices of what to do, or when you are asked questions about how you feel or how to do something.
- Can forget you are in a body to the extent that you can work to the point of injury.

Best Way to Express Yourself in a Detailed Manner
- To get sequential, logical, focused and organized, it is best to use writing.
- You are a natural list maker, and generally like to take notes, though you may not need to go back and read them.

Best Way to Explore Your Options and Sort Information
·The best way for you to sort something out is to think out loud with someone else, especially with someone who is a good listener and will let you go back and forth without providing the answer for you.

Best Way You Can Innovate
·The best way for you to come up with new ideas and spark the creative process is to get moving. Get up from the desk, walk around. Take time off to do some physical activity in which you can go at your own pace, like yoga, swimming, or walking while you "space out," not thinking about anything in particular.
·Driving can also be very effective, when you allow your mind to wander.

Your Most Effective Decision-making Strategies
·You tend to make decisions best by first writing about an issue, then talking out what you discovered in writing with a good listener, and noticing the effect of what you are saying in your body. Do you have a gut "yes" or "no" when you talk on one side of the issue or the other? Is there one option you'd rather move toward or away from?
·In a meeting when joint decisions are to be made, it is best if you are visually prepared--for instance, with a written memo, minutes from the last meeting, etc.--before the meeting, or at least as it begins.

Your Best Working Environment
·You may be very particular about what your physical environment looks like. You want to be able to make it look just the way you want and like being able to see what you are working on, rather than having it stored away.

Your Best Learning Process
·Manuals, directions, and textbooks were invented for you--you learn best by reading all about something first, then talking and hearing about it, hence "show and tell."
·If it is something technical, you can generally figure anything out from reading the text and looking at diagrams and then trying it on your own; you don't usually seek help from others.
·If you do get stuck, you do best showing someone else what you know, while narrating your process and having the other person then show you where you have gone wrong.

Communicating with Others
· Because you see the whole picture of something and want to convey that to others in story form with lots of visual details, you may be considered by others to be long-winded. Listeners may feel impatient and want you to "get to the point," while you believe that the story is the point.
· If you find your listener becoming impatient or spacing out, try asking your self what is the one main point, and convey that, either verbally or in writing.
· Because you are most organized visually, communicating in writing is the way you will be most linear and "to the point."

Receiving Feedback
· Most likely you prefer receiving feedback in writing--in notes, e-mails, written reports. You want most to be seen and heard, so you particularly want feedback that recognizes what you've written or created visually.
· Negative feedback is also best delivered to you in writing, with an opportunity to discuss further face-to-face.

Dealing with Conflict
· You may dislike feeling that you are being talked about behind your back. Most likely you prefer direct, truthful communication about difficult issues, and are usually willing to verbally discuss the source of conflict.
· With a particularly loaded issue, it can be effective for you to write about it to yourself first, then discuss it face-to-face.
· You should be aware that for some other patterns, verbal communication around difficult issues is very challenging so you might want to communicate exclusively in writing.

Receiving Support or Guidance
· You may need a lot of time to talk through your experiences: what you've done, how you feel, what you like, or what's hard for you. You may not fully know how you feel about anything until you talk about all sides of a given issue.
· You may dislike being told what to do. Usually, when working through something, you just want air time to figure out what to do. So when asking for support, invite the other person to sit facing you, and listen as you speak. If they must give guidance, ask them to explain things using metaphors and analogies as much as possible.
· For support, ask for clear time boundaries for accomplishing something as well as the consequences of not finishing on time.

The Best Way for You to Relax
· You tend to relax by reading or watching T.V. or movies, and listening to music of your choosing.
· To really relax and get a sense of what you are feeling in your body, it helps to be alone in a room and move slowly to music with your eyes closed. Or, if it feels safe, try getting a massage with music.

To Enhance Your Physical Well-being
· You may have a difficult time with a regular exercise regimen. You do best with physical activities that are not too repetitive and can be done at your own rhythm--walking, swimming, yoga, biking--since it can be challenging to motivate yourself to work out at all.
· One way to encourage movement is to find a partner to do such activities with, as long as they will not try to push you too fast or too far.
· Another option that works is to listen to a fascinating interview or dialogue on tape while moving.

Working and Communicating with Other Patterns

 **KVAs**
· KVAs tend to be very independent workers who can grasp physical and technical tasks quickly. Refrain from showing and telling them what to do; they generally prefer to figure things out on their own.
· Allow for a great deal of silence when working with a KVA and try not to answer their questions but encourage them to answer for themselves.
· Don't assume you know what they are feeling by their faces. KVA's faces go flat when they are listening or speaking. That doesn't mean they are bored or don't like you.
· Use e-mail rather than verbal communication as much as possible.
· If you are their supervisor, give them as much independence as you can and communicate as much as possible in writing, particularly if it is something important.

 **KAVs**
· People whose minds use this pattern are natural partners for you, particularly in metaphoric thinking. They are good at moving your big picture ideas into concrete action.
· Be careful not to overwhelm them with visual information--communicate as much as possible verbally, although if you want to praise them, a short e-mail will have a huge impact.

- As much as possible, don't force eye contact--sit next to, not across from, them so their eyes can move where they want to.
- If you find yourself in conflict with a KAV, suggest that you go for a walk to talk it out, and allow them to speak without looking at you.
- If you supervise a KAV, allow them to move around in meetings; they will be able to pay attention better and contribute more.

 VKAs

- VKAs are natural collaborators who make very good team players. They naturally meet you in the visual world--how things look is very important to them as well.
- Communicate as much as possible in writing--e-mail, written memos, letters.
- If you supervise a VKA, be aware that they are very auditorily sensitive so choose your words carefully!

AKVs

- AKVs are visually sensitive, so avoid too much visual information--e-mails, faxes, written memos, visual directions, or a great deal of metaphors.
- Don't draw diagrams when speaking to them, unless you want them to be very innovative in their thinking.
- Allow them not to make eye contact with you.
- If you supervise an AKV, suggest that they get up and move around as they feel inclined, even in meetings; it will enable them to know what really matters to them and have patience with those who speak more slowly.

AVKs

- AVKs are usually comfortable work partners for you, particularly in a brainstorming situation when ideas are flying. They are very good at seeing the big picture and the details, which can help bring your visions into reality.
- If there are no other patterns on the team, however, there may be a slowness in moving into action or a struggle to discover what, concretely, to do.

Famous people who use the VAK pattern:

Martin Luther King
used this pattern. He told stories to inspire others; he spoke in colorful metaphors and painted a vivid picture of his vision. He stood very still while speaking. He was a voracious reader.

Oprah Winfrey
uses this pattern. She makes extended, direct eye contact with her guests, and she sits very still through interviews. Her face expresses whatever she's feeling, and how she looks is very important to her.

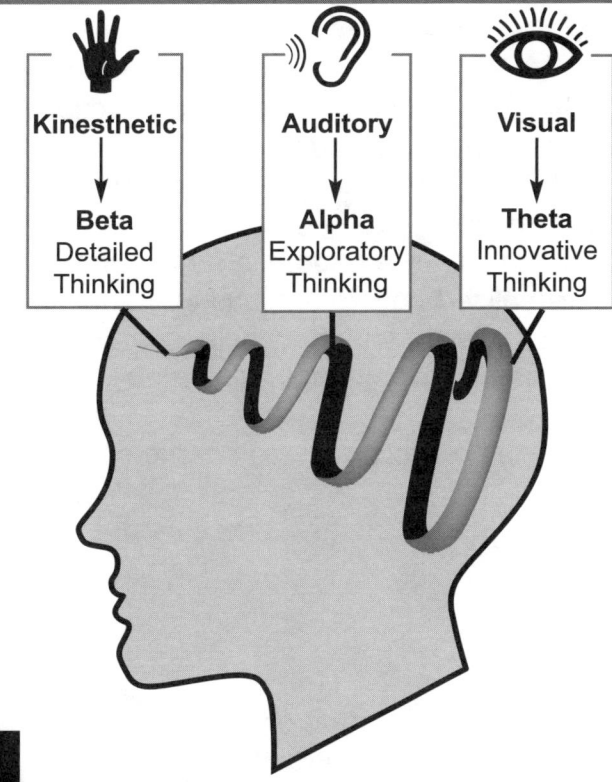

Characteristics of Your Pattern

You are very active in your body and are sensitive to too much eye contact. When given a chance, most likely you prefer to be constantly in motion. Even when sitting, you are rarely still. Your preference is to relate to the world first in some tangible way--by learning anything new experientially and hands-on. You may be a well-coordinated, "natural" athlete who likes participatory sports and seem to have an endless supply of physical energy. Physical comfort is quite important to you. You may go to great lengths to choose the clothes that have just the right weight and texture as opposed to how they look.

Touch comes naturally and easily; it is a casual but important way to connect. In general, you are keenly aware of physical sensations. You don't normally show how you feel on your face. You generally have flat facial expressions; your body speaks louder in how you stand, move, or touch.

You may use a lot of kinesthetic vocabulary--words and phrases that describe action or feeling, such as "getting a feel for," "How does that grab you?" or "I can't get a handle on it." You might end a conversation with "Catch you later," or "Let's get together soon," and frequently use kinesthetic metaphors when you speak.

Your Natural Talents and Strengths
·Physical stamina.
·Competent "doer," who prefers to be on feet and in action.
·Do things in a logical fashion. Movements are strong, steady, direct, and detailed.
·Enjoy telling stories of what you've done, how you did it and how it felt to do it.
·See the whole of something.
·An expert "finder," able to locate a needle in a haystack.
·Able to access and verbalize body sensations in a specific, organized way. Can tell exactly where your head hurts or which muscle in your leg is pulled.
·Like to work with your hands; for example, tinkering with cars, working with wood or crafts.
·Skilled at teaching people how to do things on-site since translating action into words is easy.
·May be keenly interested in how things work, everything from complex machines to the human body.

Your Challenges
·Overwhelmed by too much eye contact or visual stimulation.
·Dislike detailed visual diagrams or instructions.
·Need to move and jiggle--may have trouble sitting still for long periods of time.
·Casual touch which comes naturally to you may be offensive to others.
·May get easily bored with abstract ideas.
·Prefer to keep your eyes averted, making occasional glances to check in with the person speaking. If required to look for too long, your eyes may seem distant or glazed over.
·May act timid or tough if you are being looked at, particularly by strangers in public.
·May be a reluctant reader and writer.
·Glances that indicate judgment or criticism can be more painful than physical or verbal punishments.
·Detailed visual output--reports--can be burdensome and laborious.

Best Way to Express Yourself in a Detailed Manner
·You are the most organized and linear when you are engaged in activities that include your body.

Best Way to Explore Your Options and Sort Information
·You need to sort things by talking out loud. You may start a conversation speaking about the different choices you have, but by the end, you mostly will know which option will work best as a result of having talked it through.

Best Way You Can Innovate
·You innovate most effectively through drawing, free writing, creating big picture diagrams, daydreaming visually, or staring out a window at moving scenery when you are allowed to go at your own pace without anyone else around.

Your Most Effective Decision-making Strategies
·The best way to make a decision is to try different options and notice how each feels.
·You can also try being still and imagining each option by noticing how it feels in your body.
·Another option is to go for a walk and talk it out with a person who asks open questions and listens without giving any advice.

Your Best Working Environment
·You work best when you feel comfortable in your environment. You may go to great lengths to find the office equipment that feels just right.
·You need to do things at your own rhythm and need both contact with others and a lot of space.
·It may be challenging to sit at a desk all day. A good job for you is one that allows for a lot of motion and variety.
·If a task is kinesthetic, listening to music can help carry you forward.
·Silence may help you do a visual task.
·To do something challenging, like a visual task, it is best to be alone, for you feel the physical proximity of others and may be distracted by their presence.

Your Best Learning Process
·You learn best by doing; an apprentice- like environment.
·You may also learn well through discussion, in which you get to express your ideas and hear those of others.
·If you need instruction of some kind, it should be auditory or kinesthetic, not visual, and it should be in the moment--for example, have someone talk to you while you do the new thing.

Communicating with Others
·You are generally good at knowing what is going on for you and what you want, and are comfortable communicating with others.

- You need to be aware that not everyone is in touch with what is going on for them as well as you are, and that it may be difficult for others to communicate their feelings verbally. In that case, one solution is to have those who prefer writing e-mail you and you then respond via phone or in person.
- You may have a tendency to act first and speak later. If others seemed frightened by your abrupt movements or actions, or if you tend to express yourself physically instead of speaking about it, for example, ask people to encourage you to walk with you or do something physical--tossing a ball, or throwing rocks in a river-and then wait and listen for the words that will come.

Receiving Feedback
- Since you are visually sensitive, written feedback can leave a lasting impression. In general, it's best to receive negative feedback auditorily, preferably while in motion.
- The person giving the feedback should be sensitive to the looks they give while delivering the message.
- Positive feedback for you may include a pat on the back, a look of gratitude, a smile, or short written notes or cards.

Dealing with Conflict
- In general, you are very moved by your own feelings and when you are upset about something, it's usually easy for others to tell.
- You generally don't sit on your feelings, but tend to want to clear the air. You do it best verbally while in motion--taking a walk, or going on a run.
- When dealing with people of other patterns around a highly-charged issue, you should remember that writing is a more comfortable mode for some people, particularly when there is conflict.

Receiving Support or Guidance
- You may feel supported when people do activities with you and tell you they appreciate what you do and how well you do it.
- Those that are giving support or guidance should not insist that you sit still, but keep in mind that moving and fidgeting help you to stay alert.
- Suggest that you talk while doing something: walking, fixing the Xerox machine, working out in a company gym.
- Having something to hold and play with in your hands may also help you pay attention, as will physical proximity and standing or sitting side by side instead of face to face.
- If you need guidance, ask your helper to speak to you in action or feeling words; explain things in terms of how to do something, how it works, or how it might feel.

The Best Way for You to Relax
· You generally relax by doing something intensely physical, then sitting still and listening to music.
· If you really want to relax, watching the right T.V. show or movie can be good, although it must be exactly right, because you are very sensitive to what you see.

To Enhance Your Physical Well-being
· You are naturally in touch with your physical well-being and love to do sports of all kinds.
· However, you can, if you get injured or as you age, have difficulty knowing how to be less active and may sink into inertia or even depression. You should be encouraged to cultivate receptive kinesthetic forms, such as yoga, receiving a massage, free dancing, and find other ways to be in a body besides as Mr. or Ms. Macho.

Working and Communicating with Other Patterns

 KVAs
· People whose minds use this pattern are great partners in doing with you. You can work well together in concrete projects of all sorts.
· Because KVAs are auditorily sensitive, communicate visually as much as possible and don't expect them to be able to tell you what is going on for them.
· If you supervise a KVA, suggest they take notes or construct a model while listening in order to pay more focused attention.

VKAs
· VKAs can be exciting work partners for you because their strength is in visual detail, while yours is kinesthetic detail.
· Be aware that VKAs have sensitive ears, however, and communicate visually, particularly for important information, whenever possible.

VAKs
· People whose minds use this pattern are natural partners for you, particularly in metaphoric thinking.
· They are good at creating the big picture that you can then move into concrete action, and you may be excited about the prospect of helping manifest a dream or vision of theirs.

- The best way for the two of you to communicate is verbally; otherwise VAKs can easily overwhelm you with visual detail.
- Remember that VAKs may have trouble doing concrete things in as systematic a way as you do and that they may have trouble estimating how much time something will take.

 AKVs

- Since you are both visually sensitive, you meet most comfortably in the auditory and kinesthetic worlds.
- Go out and do things together and communicate verbally.

AVKs

- AVKs can be challenging for you because doing any physical task, even changing a light bulb, can be extremely difficult for an AVK. They generally live in the world of theory, while you love the concrete world of action.
- You can become an ally of an AVK by helping them move their ideas into specific action, particularly if you are sensitive to the awkwardness they feel in doing anything kinesthetic.

Famous people who use the KAV pattern:

Michael Jordan

uses this pattern. He is very steady and assertive with his physical energy and gestures. He is obviously very competitive physically. His facial expression is usually fairly flat, and he rarely makes steady eye contact.

Mother Teresa

used this pattern. She was constantly "doing:" hands-on, helping people. Her eyes were often downcast while she spoke. She was very energetic physically. She was known for her phrase "Do small things with great love."

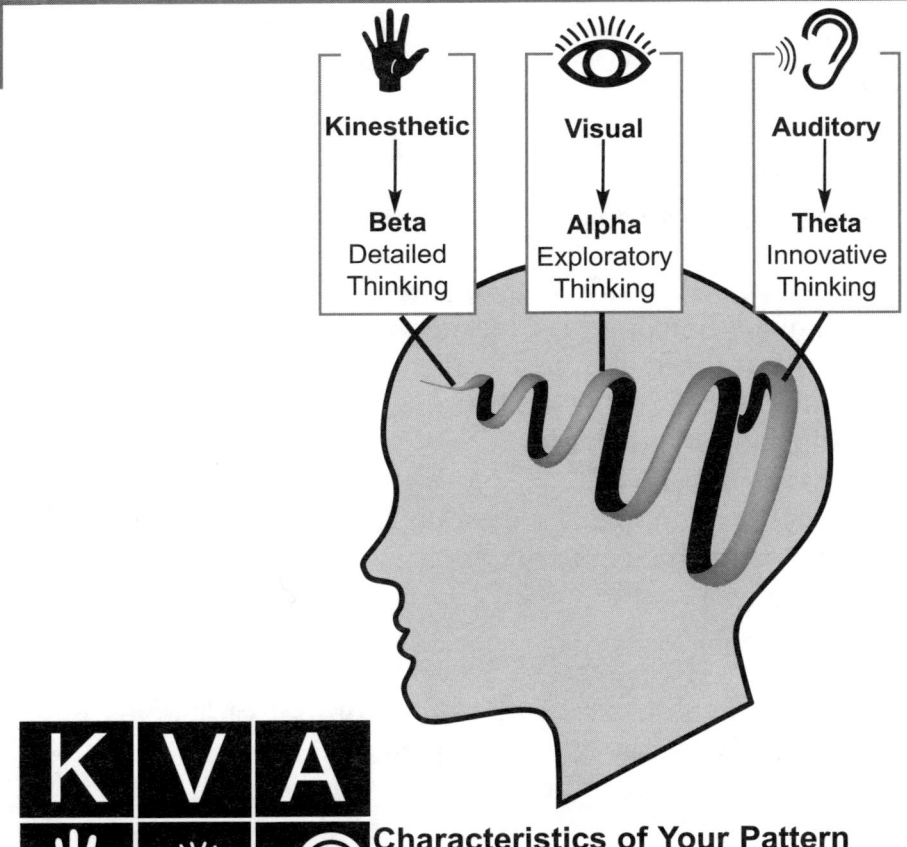

Characteristics of Your Pattern

You are soft-spoken and private with a grounded physical presence. To others you may seem to be surrounded by a deep silence. You may be interested in seemingly diverse things-football and art, for instance, or sewing and chemistry. You seem to have an intuitive sense of how it all fits together.

You are generally very aware of the specific sensations in your body. You know very clearly, for instance, if your back is sore or if a clothes tag is rubbing. You tend to choose clothes that are comfortable and allow freedom of movement, with secondary awareness of how they look.

In general, you prefer to be alone or with one or two others rather than be a part of a large social gathering. If you are in a group, you will often look for a quiet place to sit back, watch, and listen. Often labeled shy, you enjoy working or playing alone or with one close friend, and often find it easier to relate to animals or nature than to people. Your eyes can glaze over if you listen to too many words, and your facial expression usually goes flat when you speak.

You frequently use a lot of kinesthetic vocabulary, words that convey action or feelings, like "grab," "hold," "soft," or "move," and phrases like "That feels right," or "I'll be in touch soon."

Your Natural Gifts and Strengths
- Incredibly good listener who asks deep and meaningful questions.
- Do things logically.
- Can make three-dimensional images with your eyes open.
- Are able to see things from many perspectives, including the validity of many sides of an issue.
- Can see the whole of something as well its details.
- Hear the whole of something--hear harmonies.
- Can spend long periods in action.
- May have good eye-hand coordination and like working with your hands. Are easily able to put things together, sometimes in very creative ways.
- Can acquire new physical skills with ease.

Your Challenges
- May be uncomfortable speaking in a detailed way to large groups of people.
- May forget names and initials, words may take a long time to access and there may be long pauses between your words.
- Casual chitchat is awkward and difficult. Don't like to talk off the top of your head, and may freeze if pressured to speak.
- Dislike having your words filled in by others.
- May get overwhelmed by too many words.
- Very sensitive to tones of voice.
- May have difficulty expressing your emotions in words.
- When angry, you tend to withdraw.

Best Way to Express Yourself in a Detailed Manner
- You are most logical, detailed, and organized when doing something or in movement. You like doing many tasks at once.

Best Way to Explore Your Options and Sort Information
- Writing helps you know what is most important to you and what you really want to do.
- You can also try going somewhere by yourself and talking out loud about the issue, or speaking to a trusted friend who will let you "swirl" without trying to impose meaning or order on your words.

Your Most Effective Decision-making Strategies
·You make the best decisions when you are allowed to physically experiment with the various options and notice how each makes you feel rather than abstractly thinking of each one. Then, armed with that concrete information from your body, journal about the decision. Usually when you talk about a decision you've already made up your mind.
·If you need to make a snap decision in the moment and cannot physically attempt the options, try this: Get completely still, look to the side of your dominant hand, and wait to see what image emerges.

Your Best Working Environment
·You generally work best alone, or in a small group of people you know well, with little supervision or interaction from others needed.
·When a team does come together, having hands-on models to work with while discussing helps a great deal in engaging you fully.
·Your physical comfort is quite important and so you may go to great lengths to find the right chair or the right position to sit in.
·It is also crucial that you be surrounded by silence in order to work. Loud noises of any sort--even laughter--can be very challenging. If it is impossible to have an office by yourself with a door that closes, it may be somewhat effective to wear earphones so that you can choose what you listen to, usually instrumental music.
·Headset phones are a great tool, so you can walk around while having to be on long calls.
·The best way for you to pay attention in meetings is to take notes, move around, or play with something in your hands. Try being the recorder or creating a three-dimensional model of what is being discussed.

Your Best Learning Process
·You learn most easily by doing and watching and only occasionally asking questions. What this usually means is that it's best to be left alone to experiment with something until you figure it out.
·If you can't figure it out on your own, read just enough or look at a diagram or another person doing it in order to get what you need to move forward. Listening to lectures or long verbal instructions can be very difficult.

Communicating with Others
· You need to feel safe, accepted, and listened to in order to enter deeply into conversation.
· Ask others, in writing, to give you as much room to speak as possible.
· Be aware that other people aren't as verbally sensitive as you and try not to take their tone of voice or phrasing personally.
· Whenever possible, communicate with others in writing--e-mail, notes, memos--especially if you want to express your feelings.
· Suggest that in meetings with a lot of verbal back and forth, there be a time for silence to write things down and then read what you have written.

Receiving Feedback
· Most likely, you are affected deeply by what is said to you. Harsh or critical phrases can echo in your mind for years. Therefore, feedback, particularly negative feedback, should be written, not spoken; and you should be allowed to respond in writing as well.

Dealing with Conflict
· This is an area that can be difficult for you, for most likely you avoid conflict of any sort by withdrawing and churning it internally.
· If someone comes at you with a problem or conflict, suggest that he or she write to you and that you will respond visually by a certain predetermined date.
· If you find yourself stewing internally over someone, e-mail or write a note that goes something like this: I am imagining X. Is that true?

Receiving Support or Guidance
· You want to be joined in activity and adventure, and to be appreciated for what you know how to do.
· Let people know that the most effective support begins with doing something together, out in nature if possible. This is where your natural leadership style comes out.
· Let others know you need some space when you withdraw and that they shouldn't prod verbally. Suggest they try a silent pat on the back, a hand on the shoulder, or a note.
· When giving you guidance, helpers should avoid chitchat or small talk. Rather, they should ask you to talk about your experiences that may bear on the issue at hand.
· Remind others that when they ask you a question, you need silent time to think.

- You tend to not like to be told what you think or have your sentences finished for you. You should remind others to listen all the way through, even if they think they know what you are going to say.
- You tend to navigate through life by asking endless questions, looking for possibilities, and living out the answers. No matter how much people offering help are tempted, they should not answer these questions. Rather, they should help bring the attention back to you by just being silent or answering with an honest "I don't know."

The Best Way for You To Relax
- You can relax by taking long slow walks alone, listening to mellow music and staring out the window; or by having a massage with background music.

To Enhance Your Physical Well-being
- You may have a tendency to overdo physical activity. Try to balance receptive (stretching, massage, etc.) and active physical activity.
- Mostly likely you know how you feel in your body, and just need to find the ways to alleviate tension and be aware of the areas you are stressing.
- You may get bored doing the same sport over and over again, so learning new sports, or playing a competitive game once in a while is exciting.

Working and Communicating with Other Patterns

 **KAVs**
- KAVs are great partners in doing for you. You work well together in concrete projects of all sorts.
- Because they are visually sensitive, communicate as much as possible verbally.
- If you supervise a KAV, allow them to move around in meetings; they will be able to pay attention better and contribute more.

 **VKAs**
- VKAs are natural collaborators who make very good work partners for you.
- Because you are both auditorily sensitive, you tend not to offend or upset one another with your words and you both are comfortable communicating in writing as well as speaking to one another.
- You do well creating things together, with VKAs helping you concretely visualize your ideas.

VAKs
- VAKs can be challenging to you, for you may see these natural storytellers and salespeople as exaggerating or being too flamboyant verbally.
- It helps to remember that others are very inspired by these show and tellers, and that seeing the big picture, which VAKs do so well, is as vital to any team as your ability to make something happen.
- Ask them to communicate visually with you as much as possible to minimize the effect on your ears.

AKVs
- With their quick-tongued sarcasm, AKVs can be unintentionally wounding to you, but their verbal acuity can also be quite compelling and mesmerizing.
- AKVs are visually sensitive, so communicate verbally as much as possible by phone, or face to face.
- Stand or sit next to, rather than in front of them so that they can move their eyes where they want to.
- If you supervise an AKV, suggest that they get up and move around as they feel inclined, even in meetings; it will enable them to know what really matters to them and have patience with those who speak more slowly.

AVKs
- AVKs can be verbally overwhelming to you. Ask them to communicate with you in writing, or send them e-mails and allow them to call you back with their answer.
- Remind them to give you space to speak (perhaps by a pre-arranged signal, like a raised hand) they will not be offended.
- If an AVK will give you the space and feeling of safety to speak, the two of you can be a dynamic work duo, with you taking action and he or she articulating to others what is being done.

Famous people who use the VKA pattern:

Mia Hamm
uses this pattern. On the field, she leads by example rather than vocally. Her physical presence is solid and steady. In interviews, she ponders the questions before answering; her replies are usually slow, thoughtful, and very deep and sincere.

Tiger Woods
uses this pattern. He practices and works out longer and harder than any other golfer on tour, and with a very regimented schedule. His game is all about feel and mechanics. In interviews he looks aside to ponder questions, then looks back directly to answer the question. He prefers to work and play in silence.

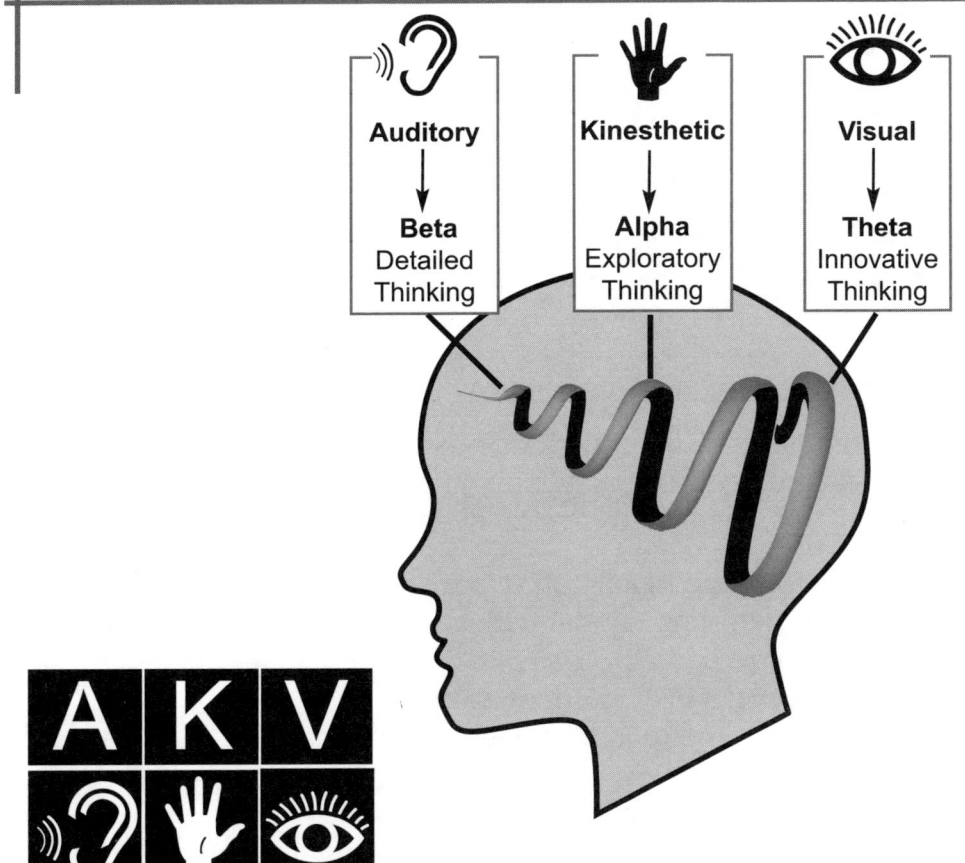

Characteristics of Your Pattern

You are extremely articulate and have a high degree of physical energy right beneath the surface. Generally, you love to take charge and tell everyone else what to do, and you love to discuss, argue, or debate anything, tell jokes, and make plays on words. You understand and make verbal inferences easily and respond quickly to spoken questions. You may have a distinctive, one-of-a-kind voice, and speak clearly, precisely and with a lot of energy, feeling, and rhythm.

It may be easy to remember what is said to you and you often can repeat what you've heard word for word, in tape-recorder fashion. This includes poetry, song lyrics, rhymes, and jokes. You may have strong feelings and opinions, which you can express easily. You seem to have an endless supply of physical energy that is not easily released. You may be well coordinated and can easily learn physical movement if mainly given verbal instruction only. You may like to participate in sports. You can be very particular about the visual images you choose--movies, television shows, and room decorations--since you are deeply influenced by what you see.

Your Natural Gifts and Strengths
·Natural leader and coach; love to tell others what to do.
·See the whole of something.
·May be a great visionary thinker.
·Love to exchange ideas verbally.
·Great at giving speeches, verbal reports, or participating in discussions of all sorts.
·Can easily find the words to teach someone else what to do.

Your Challenges
·May have trouble listening and may interrupt others, especially if you are feeling a lot of excitement.
·Can be sarcastic.
·May experience frustration when you can't create things as perfectly as you've imagined them.
·Prefer low amount of visual input; too much can overwhelm.
·Dislike detailed writing, visual diagrams, or instructions.
·Usually sensitive to prolonged eye contact.
·Nasty looks from others can leave a lasting impression.
·May have a great deal of pent-up energy right beneath the surface.

Best Way to Express Yourself in a Detailed Manner
·You are most alert and detailed in your thinking when you are talking. Therefore, when you wish to be sequential and logical, speak, even if it is to yourself.

Best Way to Explore Your Options and Sort Information
·Movement is the best way for you to explore and sort through options. Get up, pace around the room, while feeling yourself in each option.

Best Way You Can Innovate
·You can stimulate new thinking by doodling, sketching models or staring out a window at moving scenery. Or try putting a pen or pencil in your hand and allowing yourself the freedom to express yourself without worrying about details.
·It may also help you to generate new ideas to use the images of your daydreams as starting points.

Your Most Effective Decision-making Strategies
- You may not know you've made the right decision until you try it. Take the first step in a specific direction and notice how it's working and/or how you feel.
- You tend to love pilot programs and aren't afraid to regroup and fine-tune in the middle of a project.
- If taking a decision to action is not possible, it sometimes works to imagine yourself having made a choice and how you would feel.
- You may also find it helpful to talk with others who have made the choice you are thinking about to gather information and try it on in your mind.

Your Best Working Environment
- You like to be in charge of what you do and how you do it. You may get uncomfortable quickly if confined to a desk or small space for any length of time, especially if you are asked to deal with a lot of written material.
- The best work environment is one that allows for a great deal of freedom of motion and a varied schedule.

Your Best Learning Process
- You most likely learn easily through discussion and lecture, or by talking about what to do.

Communicating with Others
- You need to recognize that other people may not be as facile at speaking as you are. Even if you feel impatient when other people speak more slowly or less to the point than you want, don't finish their sentences for them.
- Try to allow for silence so that others feel they too have an opportunity to talk.
- To listen more comfortably, consider getting up and moving around or going for a walk with the other person.
- Be aware that sarcasm can be misunderstood by people of other thinking patterns who may take you literally.
- Also be aware that others may be frightened or alienated by the energy with which you speak.

Receiving Feedback
- You prefer verbal, direct, to-the-point feedback.
- You may appreciate it most when it is as humorous as possible.
- When you do write something, it's very important to you and you may prefer to have written comments on a separate page.

© PTP, INC.

Dealing with Conflict
·It's important to remember that people of other patterns may have difficulty expressing themselves verbally in highly charged situations. To deal effectively, suggest that you do something kinesthetic together while talking, such as walking. Walk in a side-by-side fashion, so you can look wherever you are comfortable.
·Consider suggesting they e-mail or write their thoughts in a clear and simple way, and then allow you to respond verbally.

Receiving Support or Guidance
·You are a natural coach and prefer to offer guidance and support to others.
·For your own support, you may want to seek individuals who have the skills you want to learn. You may be more willing to hear advice and experiential stories from those whose work you respect.
·In a team situation, most likely you want to be met by peers who share your intensity of commitment and energy.

The Best Way for You to Relax
·You may like to listen to music or go to concerts when you have leisure time.
·You may enjoy exploring on the Internet or playing computer/video games where you can get lost in the speed and number of visual choices.
·Although you can be particular about what you watch, you can really get captured by a good TV program, movie, or book, and use this as a way to wind down.
·Travel of any kind, even day trips, can be very relaxing.

To Enhance Your Physical Well-being
·You may intuitively know that you need daily exercise to manage stress.
·Team sports or interactive sports, especially those that allow for talking and verbal banter (hockey, baseball, basketball), or one-on one sports like raquetball or tennis, may be particularly enjoyable.

Working and Communicating with Other Patterns

 KVAs
·KVAs tend to be very independent workers who can grasp physical and technical tasks quickly. Refrain from telling them what to do; they generally prefer to figure things out on their own.

- Allow for a great deal of silence and try not to answer their questions but encourage them to answer for themselves.
- Avoid the temptation to finish their sentences.
- Be aware that they are very sensitive to tone of voice and can be easily wounded by something you say.
- Whenever possible, walk together when you have something important or sensitive to say.
- If you are their supervisor, give them as much independence as you can and communicate as much as possible in writing, particularly if it is something important.

 KAVs

- The two of you are natural collaborators in doing. Talk about your joint vision.
- Get specific to avoid frustration. You both tend to have images of the way things are supposed to look when complete. Make sure you are going for the same thing.
- If you agree to move ahead on a task, give them time to do things their own way first, and then respond to their questions and offer feedback. Allow them the opportunity to explore different options out loud before drawing conclusions.
- If you supervise a KAV, allow them to move around in meetings; they will be able to pay attention better and contribute more.

VKAs

- VKAs are natural collaborators who make very good team players.
- They may talk in circles and ask a great deal of questions that you should refrain from answering. Rather, say something like, "What a good question. What do you think?"
- Try not to interrupt or finish their sentences for them.
- When it is really important, communicate as much as possible in writing--e-mail, written memos, letters.
- If you supervise a VKA, be aware that they are very auditorily sensitive so choose your words and tone of voice carefully.

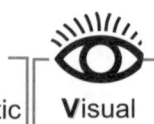

VAKs

·The two of you share the ability and desire to speak passionately about what matters to you.
·Join forces with a VAK and you may have an ally who can communicate succinctly and specifically in writing in ways that could be difficult for you.
·VAKs find taking notes and making lists the easiest way to keep track of what is said in meetings and what needs to be done for follow-up.
·They may need written instructions or time to talk through a task to make sure expectations are clear before beginning it.

AVKs

·You meet naturally in verbal repartee, but be aware that when the two of you get going, you could take up all the air space in a meeting.
·AVKs are kinesthetically sensitive, so avoid casual contact--punches on the arm, pats on the shoulder, etc.,--and be aware that doing anything physical can be extremely challenging for them.

Famous people who use the AKV pattern:

Robin Williams
uses this pattern. He is very energetic, first with his words, then with his body language. He can talk for hours without visual cues (just watch his stand-up routine) but never stays still for one minute. He seems to dress for comfort rather than appearance. He seldom makes eye contact, either in interviews or in the roles he plays.

Madonna
uses this pattern. She also speaks and sings with a great deal of energy. Her concerts are fraught with action and frenzied energy and dancing. She always makes a splash when she talks, and is often sarcastic. She seems to look through or over people when talking to them, and doesn't hold eye contact for long.

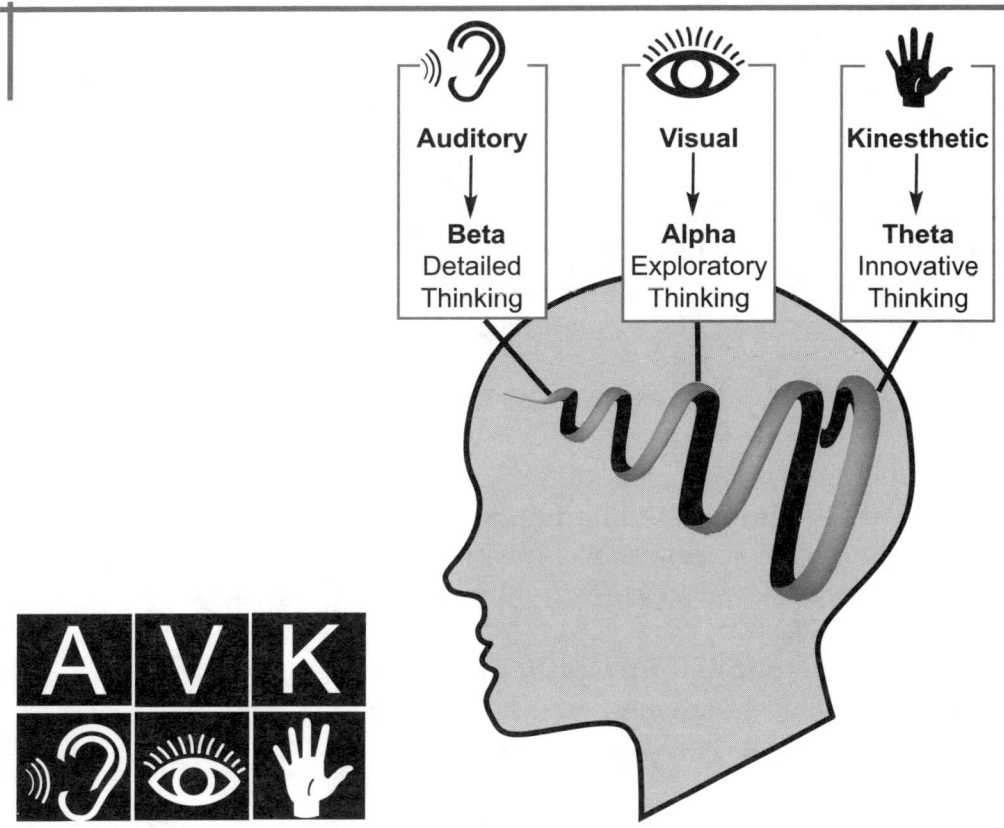

Characteristics of Your Pattern

You are often considered "smart" because you can easily verbalize what you think and keep up with the pace of any conversation. Your words pour out in logical order without hesitation in a straightforward manner. You tend to speak in statements rather than questions. The content of your speech is largely conceptual, and your vocabulary is relatively abstract and detailed; you may love verbal humor, facts, history, and ideas of all kinds. You may be fascinated with language and can often learn to speak other languages with ease. Most likely you enjoy explaining, debating, discussing, and arguing almost anything. You may frequently use words and phrases like "hear," "say," "sounds like," "That rings a bell," "Let's play it by ear," and "Talk to you soon."

Your Natural Gifts and Strengths
·Love to exchange ideas verbally.
·Great at giving speeches, verbal reports, or participating in all sorts of discussions.
·Able to see the big picture and the details of a project simultaneously.
·Remember precisely what was said.

·Usually a good reader and writer, though talking is your preferred mode.

Your Challenges
·Often extremely shy about expressing your feelings or being touched.
·Tend to hate physical humor, such as tickling, pranks, or practical jokes.
·Can have trouble doing hands-on, technical skills.
·May be awkward with mechanical devices of all sorts.
·May have a tendency to interrupt others in meetings and monopolize conversations.
·Can forget entirely that you have a body and can work to the point of injury without noticing it.

Best Way to Express Yourself in a Detailed Manner
·You are most alert and detailed in your thinking when you are talking. Therefore, when you wish to be sequential and logical, speak, even if it is to yourself.

Best Way to Explore Your Options and Sort Information
·When you are reading, writing, or drawing, you are best able to compare, explore, or think "on the one hand, on the other hand." Therefore, the most effective way to explore options is in writing.
·If you find yourself stuck and going between "either/or", try writing out both sides of the argument on two different notepads, with each pad representing one side.

Best Way You Can Innovate
·The best way to come up with new ideas and spark the creative process is to get moving. Get up from the desk, walk around, go for a ride. Take time off to do yoga or go swimming or for a walk while you "space out," not thinking about anything in particular.

Your Most Effective Decision-making Strategies
·Most likely the best way for you to make a decision is to talk about it with others first, getting as much information as possible, then read about it, and, finally, write down all the pros and cons.
·It is often effective to think metaphorically about the problem at hand: Is it like a boulder? An iceberg? Then let it sit for a few days while you put it out of your mind. The answer will often come out of nowhere when you are doing something physical--in the shower, for instance, or driving the car.
·If you must make a snap decision in the moment, try this: Get completely quiet, look to the side that your dominant hand is on, and wait to see what pops into your mind.

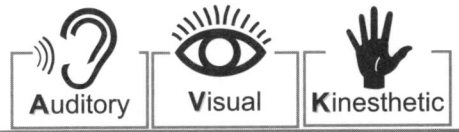

Your Best Working Environment
- You tend not to be particularly sensitive to your physical work environment, although you may be easily distracted by others' conversations and want to join in.
- You may like to do as much work as possible over the phone and can sit still for long periods of time.
- You can work alone, but like to have the chance for verbal interactions throughout the day. If you spend too much time reading or at the computer, you may become verbally "pent up."

Your Best Learning Process
- You learn best through discussion, then reading.
- When stuck, you do best to get someone to explain verbally and, particularly if it's a technical or physical skill, to demonstrate how to do it while explaining verbally at the same time, while you take notes. Then try it out immediately after on your own and at your own pace.

Communicating with Others
- You need to recognize that others are not as facile with language as you are. Don't finish other people's sentences and try to allow for silent pauses so that others feel they have a chance to talk.
- To listen more comfortably, ask the other person to give you a topic headline--"I want to talk to you about the deadline for this project."
- To communicate something that expresses feelings, consider doing it in writing. It may be easier to express feelings visually rather than verbally.

Receiving Feedback
- Verbal communication--whether face-to-face or on the phone is the most effective way to receive any kind of feedback.
- Most likely you prefer "direct" communication--you don't like to feel that the other person is holding back or candy-coating criticism. If the feedback is negative, it is best that it be verbal and very direct.
- If the feedback is positive, it tends to be more effective to receive it in writing, for written communication is felt more deeply than verbal.

Dealing with Conflict
- While people of this pattern tend to be more comfortable verbally in conflict than others, it helps to remember that people of other patterns may have difficulty expressing themselves verbally in highly charged situations. Suggest that people of other patterns e-mail or write their thoughts, and ask how they would like to proceed after you've read their communication.

Receiving Support or Guidance
- Doing something physical, even something seemingly as simple as changing the paper in the copy machine, can be challenging and you may need to be shown the same thing several times.
- You may not do well with others watching while you learn to do something. Let others know of your need for privacy and to move at your own pace, which may be slow, when learning something that's hands-on. Explain that you learn best if they demonstrate while talking, and then leave you alone to try it for yourself, and be on call to repeat if necessary.
- For support, ask others to remind you to take care of yourself physically and to remind you when you are interrupting.

The Best Way for You to Relax
- Typically, you unwind by reading, listening to music or lectures, or watching movies or T.V.

To Enhance Your Physical Well-being
- You may have a difficult time with a regular exercise regimen. If so, try a physical activity that is not too repetitious and can be done at your own rhythm--walking, swimming, yoga, biking--although it can be challenging to motivate yourself to move at all.
- One way to encourage movement is to find a partner to do such activities with, as long as they will not try to push you too fast or too far.

Working and Communicating with Other Patterns

 **KVAs**

- KVAs tend to be very independent workers who can grasp physical and technical tasks quickly. Refrain from telling them what to do; they generally prefer to figure things out on their own.
- Allow for a great deal of silence when working with a KVA and try not to answer their questions but encourage them to answer for themselves.
- Avoid the temptation to finish their sentences.
- Be aware that they are very sensitive to tone of voice and the words you choose to speak, and can be easily wounded by something you say.
- Use e-mail rather than verbal communication as much as possible.
- If you are their supervisor, give them as much independence as you can and communicate as much as possible in writing, particularly if it is something important.

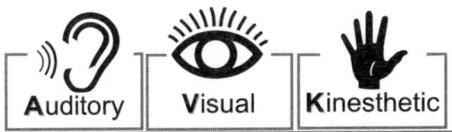

KAVs

- People whose minds use this pattern may be challenging for you because they like to do and to talk about their feelings about what they are doing, while you tend to live in the world of abstract ideas.
- Communicate as much as possible verbally, although if you want to praise them, a short e-mail will have a huge impact.
- Sit next to, not across from, them so their eyes can move where they want to.
- If you find yourself in conflict with a KAV, suggest that you go for a walk to talk it out, and allow them to speak without looking at you.
- If you supervise a KAV, allow them to move around in meetings; they will be able to pay attention better and contribute more.

VKAs

- VKAs are natural collaborators who make very good team players. They can be challenging to you because they speak in loops and circles rather than in a straight line. Don't finish their sentences for them!
- If you find yourself becoming impatient, take a deep breath and ask them to draw you a picture of what they mean.
- Communicate as much as possible in writing--e-mail, written memos, letters.
- If you supervise a VKA, be aware that they are very auditorily sensitive so choose your words carefully.

VAKs

- Usually, VAKs are comfortable work partners for you, particularly in a brainstorming situation when ideas are flying. VAKs are very good at seeing the big picture, which can be very inspiring to you, for you can then offer the details needed to make the picture a reality.
- If there are no other patterns on the team, however, there may be a slowness in moving into action or a struggle to discover what, concretely, to do.

AKVs

- The two of you meet naturally in verbal repartee, but be aware that when the two of you get going, you could take up all the air space in a meeting.
- AKVs are visually sensitive, so communicate verbally as much as possible--on the phone, or face to face.

© PTP, INC.

AVK

- Stand or sit next to, rather than in front of, them so that they can move their eyes where they want to.
- If you supervise an AKV, suggest that they get up and move around as they feel inclined, even in meetings; it will enable them to know what really matters to them and have patience with those who speak more slowly.

Famous people who use the AVK pattern:

Larry King uses this pattern. He is very pointed and direct in his questions, almost asking them as statements. His language is very precise and ornate. First he speaks, then he looks directly at his guests until they answer. He is relatively still in his body, and looks somewhat awkward when he moves.

Hillary Clinton uses this pattern. Her voice carries a certain surety and power; she speaks very directly and doesn't mince words. She stays very still as she speaks. She tends to glance away whenever she needs to think something over, then looks directly back when speaking.

Chapter VI

Frequently Asked Questions

Are there particular careers that are better suited to specific patterns?
i.e. Auditory in beta - lawyer, radio announcer, public speaker.
Visual in beta - architect, graphic designer, editor.
Kinesthetic in beta - athlete, physical therapist, coach.

A. What is true is that you can function in your beta mode for long periods of time, and be comfortable in this channel in the public domain. Your theta mode is your most sensitive channel and while you can still be a great in this mode, you would be more private about it, or need the right conditions to be in "public". So for example, a KVA could most obviously be a great personal trainer, but he or she could also be a great music composer, because of their sensitivity to sound and ability to hear music so deeply. An AVK could clearly be a phone coach and never get tired of the lengthy discussions; the same person could also be a choreographer because of their sensitivity to movement. Working as a professional stage dancer, while possible, would be much more difficult for them.

If auditory triggers me into theta, should I stay away from speaking in public?

A. No, of course you can do it; just make sure you are prepared in a way that works for you, such as using notes, or allowing yourself to move or play with coins in your pocket. This would help your words flow naturally, whereas it would be more challenging for you to just stand still in front of a large crowd and speak.

Is someone for whom kinesthetic triggers theta commonly lazy?

A. No. Lazy is the wrong term. They can forget they are in a body, and for them to do physical activity requires the right environment and comfort level.

I feel like I could equally be triggered into beta by visual *and* auditory. What are the common differentiators?

A. Which one could you do for longer? Which one could you be active and receptive in at the same time? Which one are you least distractable in?
For example if auditory comes first you could be talking on the phone and listening to an external conversation at the same time. If visual comes first you could read and watch TV simultaneously, handling multitudes of visual input without feeling distracted.

Frequently Asked Questions

Does the school system favor a particular pattern?

A. Generally yes, and it depends on the culture or region. Most U.S. classrooms favor the VAK or AVK pattern. (Show and tell). Even colleges tend towards lectures-sit, listen and look at your book. Some pre-schools and kindergartens are getting more experiential, such as the Montessori schools.

Is one pattern better than another?

A. Each pattern has its own strengths and challenges. You can accomplish anything in any pattern; understanding your pattern will accelerate your learning curve and help you accomplish a task more fruitfully.

Do some patterns work together better than others?

A. Knowing about the patterns can help you relate with **anyone** *better. Communication simpatico can mean you are using a common perceptual channel to create a good relationship. The opposite, a relationship breakdown, can be a pattern mismatch where one person is communicating through one channel that is challenging for another.*
For example: A boss who uses the AVK pattern is giving criticism verbally to an employee who uses the VKA pattern. It has a negative effect on the employee, who becomes defensive and withdraws--not because of the content of the criticism, but because of the mode of delivery. If the boss had written an e-mail to the employee, the criticism would most likely have been more effective.

Does your pattern dictate your personality traits?

A. An emphatic "No." There are common characteristics that have to do with thought processes, but they completely different than personality.

If I tend to space out when someone is talking, does it mean auditory triggers me into theta?

A. Generally yes, especially if you are not moving, or have no visual support.

Quick Reference

VAK

Characteristics:
- Love to read
- Steady eye contact
- Can sit still for long periods
- Energetic conversationally, speak in stories

Guidelines: For working with the VAK pattern
- Show first, then tell stories and use metaphors
- Use colorful visuals to explain
- Avoid competitive physical activity
- Give feedback visually first, then talk it out

VKA

Characteristics:
- Take longer to speak their opinions
- Learn experientially, hands on
- Systematic in doing

Guidelines: For working with the VKA pattern
- Give them time to speak; avoid interrupting
- Use visuals to help explain, or come to a decision
- Encourage them to move as they speak
- Give feedback visually

KAV

Characteristics:
- Action-oriented
- Doing comes first
- Eye shy, overwhelmed with visual details

Guidelines: For working with the KAV pattern
- Encourage physically first
- Best communication when moving/doing
- Avoid staring or showing a lot visuals
- Give feedback walking and talking

KVA

Characteristics:
- Often ponder their words before speaking
- Learn experientially, hands on
- Systematic in doing

Guidelines: For working with the KVA pattern
- Allow silence between words
- Avoid interrupting
- Use visuals to help explain
- Give feedback visually, giving them time to respond

AVK

Characteristics:
- Speak logically about facts, ideas, concepts
- Can sit for hours without moving
- Look at you first, then away
- Great at verbal recall

Guidelines: For working with the AVK pattern
- Tell and show first; give them a verbal headline
- Touch and physical activity not casual
- Give feedback verbally

AKV

Characteristics:
- Like verbal directing and using humor
- Speak with energy and volume
- Eye shy, overwhelmed with too much visual detail

Guidelines: For working with the AKV pattern
- Be direct verbally
- Encourage to talk
- Avoid a lot of visual information
- Give feedback verbally, while they can move

How this Information Has Helped:
Quotes from people who have learned about personal thinking patterns

"This information is like a secret weapon. It gives you a huge advantage in effective communication and successful negotiation."

"This explains why I gravitated towards certain kinds of courses in school. My success had as much to do with the delivery style as the subject matter."

"The true measure of productivity for me is not in the hours I log at my desk anymore. To be truly effective, I now understand my need to move around to stimulate innovation."

"Public speaking comes a lot more easily to me knowing ways in which I can reduce my nervousness and engage my audience."

"My perception of eye contact has changed significantly. I no longer assume someone is sneaky if they don't steadily look me in the eye."

"I am no longer mortally offended when my colleague interrupts me. It's her way of actually paying attention to what I am saying."

"I was so frustrated by my husband's hesitance to talk about our issues and so busy filling in his words, that I missed what he was really trying to say."

"My boss was so meticulous about detail that everyone in the office complained about his micro-management. Now we understand why visual detail is of such primary importance. We don't take it personally anymore and can work without resenting him for it."

"My tolerance for staff meetings has increased immensely now that I understand ways to best focus my attention and keep engaged."

"How did I ever get along without knowing this before? Everyone should learn this!"

"This information is so obvious, but incredibly powerful. It can be applied to all facets of my life."

"I no longer waste energy comparing myself to others. Instead I notice and appreciate our different abilities and styles."

"This information is a great way to truly 'know thyself.'"

"You can learn something in a fraction of the time if you recognize the optimum conditions of how to learn best. It has saved me literally hundreds of hours of frustration."

"I used to think I was a hopeless speller, and get really down on myself about it. Now I understand why visual information can sometimes slip through the cracks."

"I finally understand why I dread talking on the phone! I would much rather e-mail someone instead."

"I have two kids and the differences in the way they learn sometimes made me wonder if they were from the same planet, let alone the same family. Now it all makes sense."

"This information shatters the assumptions that I made about everyone I work with. It opened the flood gates of effective communication."

"Don't make me sit in a chair and listen; I won't remember what you say. Take me on a walk and talk to me, and I'll remember what you say for the rest of my life."

"This is why having the right romantic atmosphere is so important to my wife; she is so sensitive to her environment."

What Kids Say:

"My dad and mom are the only ones allowed to hug me. Anyone else--YUK!"

"My teacher is always telling me to sit, and everyone says I am hyper-active. Now I can tell everyone 'I need to move' and explain why!"

"Don't ask my mom to do it, she not good at making things like me, but she talks well."

"Now I know why I talk a lot. Not everyone likes talking so much, but I do."

Chapter VII
About Professional Thinkig Partners:
Our Programs and Products

As a result of understanding Personal Thinking Patterns, we hope that you will be able to recognize, develop, and utilize your unique talents. In our experience, every domain of communication is enhanced by understanding thinking patterns, including sales and marketing, articulating the company vision, communicating with boards and shareholders, collaborative thinking among team members, and overall individual respect and self-esteem. It helps each person recognize how they can contribute to the overall success of the company.

In multi-ethnic and multicultural environments, this understanding also helps us bridge the gap and find common ground in rifts that traditionally have been attributed to gender, race, and culture. Often communication gaps are caused by a lack of understanding of the different ways we process information, as well as the assumption that "different" implies a deficit. By understanding this information, evaluations will be based on merit and true performance. This will enhance a company's ability to attract, retain, and develop talented individuals.

About Professional Thinking Partners:

Professional Thinking Partners (PTP) is an international consulting firm based in Utah and California. PTP designs and delivers custom programs for global corporations, governments, non-profits and individuals to develop human capital and to create collaborative cultures and communities.

What We Value: All Who Are Different Belong
The core of our work is the expansion of human capacity. Our intent is to maximize the contribution possible for each individual, and to help great minds think together.

PTP Programs for Corporations:

Diversity In Thinking
We aspire to help organizations treat their people as assets rather than deficits, and guide them in developing the conditions that maximize innovative thinking and the liberation of human capacity. PTP offers one and two-day programs that focus on understanding Diversity of Thinking. This understanding helps us recognize that people have different ways of processing information, approaching problems, and communicating with one another. We explore Personal Thinking Patterns in-depth, and expand understanding and applicability by incorporating the thinking models that describe the "software" of the brain.

The Collaborative Edge: Developing Higher Performing Teams

Research tells us that one of the key capacities leaders must have in order to face the demands of complexity is the ability to integrate the expertise of various players who think in essentially different ways to anticipate emerging futures and find innovative solutions. This, according to Michael Lipson, Professor of Economics at Columbia University "requires expanding our capacity to be creative, to concentrate and improvise, and to learn together." The Collaborative Edge, a dynamic and interactive three day workshop, has been created to meet this need. We take real work issues and provide a variety of skills and processes to help participants think and act together across cultural and other divides to increase performance, enjoyment and learning in your organization.

PTP Clients Include:

AT&T Broadband, Royal Dutch/Shell, British Petroleum, The Coca-Cola Company, The US Navy, The Government of Nigeria, The Government of Canada, Hewitt Associates, The Sundance Institute, DaimlerChrysler, EDS, Street-Works, SciVentures, Canyon Ranch, and professional and amateur athletes.

Other Products that Support this Book:

The Mind Museum computer software assessment.
A CD-ROM and web-based interactive multimedia application that allows users to discover their Personal Thinking Pattern. The Mind Museum is the first assessment of its kind to employ multi-modal questions, experiences and stimuli to determine the best way for individuals to learn, interact and communicate with others. Users journey through a variety of 'rooms' in a virtual museum, each using a combination of video, animation, hands-on experiments and text-based topics to build an overall learning pattern for the user.

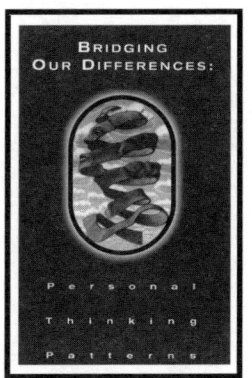

Bridging Our Differences: Personal Thinking Patterns (video).

This video graphically depicts the six thinking patterns. By showing groups representing each of the six patterns in action, the video highlights the differences in learning, communicating, and problem-solving between the groups, as well as offering suggestions for working with people who use each pattern.

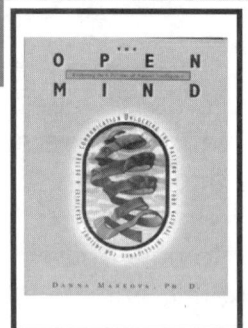
The Open Mind: Exploring the Six Patterns of Natural Intelligence, by Dawna Markova. Dr. Markova, who holds Ph.D's. in education and psychology, has spent over thirty years teaching people how to learn and communicate with confidence. In this important book, she explains the six distinct ways we think and teaches readers how to identify their pattern and communicate most effectively. Every one of us has a special genius and the discovery of yours is the key to faster learning and better communication.

An Unused Intelligence: Physical Thinking for 21st Century Leadership, by Andy Bryner and Dawna Markova. The hottest topic in business today is learning--with learning organization founder Peter Senge leading the way. This groundbreaking business book teaches how to think differently about chronic problems and offers simple physical exercises that people in business can do individually or with partners and teams to enhance their ability to work creatively and collaboratively.

Our Work with Kids:

PTP is working alongside Impactanation, a Toronto-based firm, to co-design one-day programs for the youth market and for families. These programs will launch in Canada, the United States, and the Netherlands starting in the fall of 2002.

Youth programs:
The most valuable gift we can give to our children is the understanding of how they learn and the recognition of their talents and capacities. The youth workshop gives them an "operating manual" to their own minds.

Young people learn to identify their thinking patterns in a one-day interactive and highly energized team environment. They develop their ability to identify other learning styles and they go home with strategies to help them with school/homework, relationships, and other areas of interest based on their own unique learning style.

Following the program, interested youth become engaged in internships to become trainers of other young people who are interested in learning about their thinking patterns.